The Brown Mama Mindset

A Blueprint for Black Moms on Life, Love & Home

The Brown Mama Mindset

A Blueprint for Black Moms on Life, Love & Home

Muffy Mendoza

Copyright © 2018 by Muffy Mendoza

All rights reserved. No part of this publication may be reproduced, distributed or transmitted in any form or by any means, without prior written permission.

Cover design by Soleil Meade
Editing by Teresa R. Hunt

ISBN-13: 978-1987591835
ISBN-10: 1987591836

Dedication

This book is dedicated to the two people who helped me love home. My mother, for trying her best to make a home for me and my husband for being my home.

Contents

Foreword 11

Introduction 17

SECTION I: LIFE 27

Chapter 1: Time Race................................. 29

Chapter 2: Nourished Roots 47

Chapter 3: Stop Losing Your Keys 59

Chapter 4: Accept Your Exceptionalism ... 77

Chapter 5: Joy Reservoir............................. 89

SECTION II: HOME 103

Chapter 6: Be Pretty.................................. 105

Chapter 7: The Little Things 117

Chapter 8: Make it Smell Good................ 131

Chapter 9: God Space 145

Chapter 10: Routine & Ritual...................163

Section III: LOVE 177

Chapter 11: Blame Game 179

Chapter 12: Insecure 199

Chapter 13: To Be Loved... 217

Chapter 14: Parenting the Black Way.....................229

Chapter 15: Sankofa 253

Reflections..267

Bibliography & Recommendations 275

Foreword

Recently, I have been thinking a lot about mothers and the important role we play in the continuation and development of humanity. If we pause for a moment, we realize that there is but one portal to arrive at this mortal coil, and that one way is through the body of a woman. It's such a humbling and terrifying thing to realize that women are the connectors between the supernatural and the natural. The passage of human beings from there to here creates one of the most special relationships humans can experience. As magical and spiritual as this reality may seem, it does not mean that motherhood is without its trials and tribulations.

When Muffy asked me to write the preface for her book, I wanted to say," No". I wanted to tell her that I've haphazardly worked my way through this motherhood thing. Although I have always been there for my daughters and have tried to afford them every opportunity that would prepare them for this world,

I often fear my introverted nature and traumatic childhood experiences could have made me less open, less transparent and more fearful of a love strong enough to rip the marrow in my bones. Because the love I have for them *is* the very marrow in my bones. I wanted to tell her that I did not have the bandwidth to homeschool, or breastfeed, or prepare organic baby food and all the other things moms are supposed to do. I wanted to tell her that I've screamed and I've hollered way more than I should have, while remembering the weight of my heart the moment my children realize how deeply flawed I am.

I wanted to tell her about the moments where we all knew that my love, although complete, was not perfect enough to protect them from everything this world will throw at them. I think about all the things I forgot to tell them, teach them and prepare them for, or all the times I tried to cram every lesson into one teachable moment, exasperating us all and forgetting the point of the lesson to begin with. If I am honest, there are still times my heart and mind are so bound by the day-to-day challenges of life that it does not leave room for the infinite amount of patience I was so certain I'd have when they rumbled in womb and I awaited their blessed arrival. Yet, our love for one another endures.

I wanted to tell her "no" because I've fallen short of model motherhood too many times to count. Instead, I swallowed my pride and inadequacies, and I told her "Yes". I said yes, not only because there isn't anything I wouldn't do for my dear friend of more than 20 years, but because it was then that I remembered Muffy already knows and my condition is probably the norm. This is why she wrote **The Brown Mama Mindset: A Blueprint for Black Moms on Life, Love & Home;** to remind Brown Mamas like myself that we are not alone and to set us free from the bondage of the perfect motherhood stereotypes.

As a young mom, I felt it was my responsibility to ensure my children looked, felt and behaved perfectly. I thought that is what the world was asking of me as a mother of Black children. Society conditions you to think perfection is the appropriate currency of motherhood, however, it is not. I now realize that delivering perfect, contributing members to society, wasn't and isn't my responsibility at all. My responsibility is simply to direct them to love: Love for self, Love for their Creator, and Love for others.

It is with this new understanding that I feel honored to serve as the preamble to this new motherhood mindset Muffy's book is sure to usher in. When Muffy created the platform for Brown Mamas a few years ago, she did it to ensure Brown Mamas didn't feel so alone on the journey through motherhood. As the founder of Pittsburgh Brown Mamas, she opened her home and her heart to a group mothers in need of comfort, rest and a reality check. Eventually, she created a virtual space, BrownMamas.com to reach more women in need of solace from a world that often lacks empathy for our plight and the plight of our children. It was right there in those groups that I began to be gentler with myself and more understanding of who I was as a woman and the role that I played in how I lived, loved and learned as a mother. Muffy's leadership, in the space of Brown motherhood, is done with the unabashed fervor of a journalism– challenging the systems and attitudes that undermine the physical safety of Black women and children. I am grateful to call her my friend and we are all blessed to have this warrior mother on our side.

This book is for every Brown Mama who has considered perfection when Love is enough.

My children retain the right to revoke their love for others should it jeopardize the love they have for themselves, or their Creator, and so do you.

-Diamonte Z. Walker

Introduction

Do Black mothers know there is a problem? When I initially thought about writing a book about the mindset of Black mothers I was certain someone had already done this. With all the books out there, that are written about Black women in corporate America, Black women and relationships, Black women and racism, Black women and money management, surely someone had written a book about the mental and emotional experience of being a Black mother in America. But, to my surprise - CRICKETS!

I'd been Goggling the words "books on Black motherhood," "books for Black moms" and all sorts of word combinations that I thought would certainly lead me to something other than books on birthing and breastfeeding, but no.

For some reason it appears few in our society have made the connection between the lack of Black women in the boardroom, the often-desperate financial gains made by Black women, and the lack of long-standing African-American male-female relationships with the equally strained experience of being a Black mother in America.

I'm not sure that as Black women we even know that there is a direct correlation between the way we view ourselves as mothers, and the moves we make daily throughout our lives.

I recently conducted a survey of over 200 Black mothers in an inner-city in the East Coast. I was actually doing the survey to find information on what type of books Black mothers like to read, and stumbled upon some startling information.

I asked the mothers, "When you have a motherhood problem what do you do?" About 11% said they would listen to a podcast, 13% said they would read a book, even less said they would go to a seminar or attend a webinar, over 65% of the moms surveyed said when they have a motherhood problem they 'just think their way out of it.'

I was floored! It dawned on me that Black women very seldom venture outside of their own circle of knowledge when attempting to remedy the problems they are faced with during the trials of raising and rearing Black children.

I run a support a group for Black moms in Pittsburgh called Pittsburgh Brown Mamas (PBM). One of the ways I communicate with our Mamas is through a private Facebook group, which engages with over 2000 Black moms in the region each week.

The moms are always posting in the PBM group to seek out advice on everything from where to buy a car seat to how to heal broken co-parenting relationships. So, I know that Black moms often rely on each other for help in sticky situations.

But, what happens when your girlfriend doesn't know the answer, or has the wrong answer? What happens when everyone in your circle is working with limited information? Or, what happens when you just can't seem to find the answer?

My mother tells a story to me quite often and it goes like this:

A young girl notices that her mother cuts off both sides of a ham and places it in a pot to season collard greens when she cooks them. She asks her mother, "Mama why do you cut off the sides of the ham before you put it in the greens?" The Mama responds, "Because that's the way the old folks do it. Besides, it gives the greens extra flavor."

Mama begins to ponder the answer to the question and decides to call Grandma. Mama calls Grandma and asks, "Mama why did you teach me to cut off the sides off the ham before I put it in the pot of greens?" Grandma responds, "Because that's how the old folks do it. It gives the greens extra flavor." Grandma begins to ponder, and realizes *she* has no idea why her Mama taught her to cut the sides off the ham before putting it in the greens, but Great Grandma has passed and she can't ask her.

Well time wanes on and Grandma and Mama pass away too. The young girl, who is now a grown woman with children of her own, is going through her Mama's belongings in the weeks after the funeral. Amongst her belongings she finds a cookbook that belonged to her great grandmother. She is excited to inherit the greens recipe perfected by her great, great grandmother. On the way home, she stops at the grocery store and gets all the ingredients.

She invites her young daughter into the kitchen to cook and places the cookbook on the counter. The young girl flicks through the pages of the cookbook. Just as her Mama is about to put the piece of meat with the sides cut off into the pot, she hears her daughter reading from the cookbook, "Don't forget to cut off the sides of the ham for the small pot."

She instantly turns around and says, "What did you say?" The young girl responds, "It says on the back of the greens recipe, "Don't forget to cut off the sides of the ham for the small pot."

Her Mama smiles a big grin, and reads in tiny print on the back page of the greens recipe:

"Don't forget to cut off the sides of the ham for the small pot."

Now how many times have we taken advice from another Mama who forgot to read the fine print? Do you see how misleading it can be to operate out of a false understanding? One small piece of information can completely change the way you view an experience, circumstance or person. All I'm saying is that we have to begin to reevaluate the mindset we use in thinking our way out of our problems.

I love that Mamas are thinking, but I know that many of us are working with cookbooks that we haven't read in their entirety. Many of us are running so fast through this thing called life that we forget to read the fine print.

Many times, our current mindsets don't allow us to see that our entire perspective, and the perspectives of those in our circle, are out of order.

The Brown Mama Mindset seeks to help Black mothers view the whole spectrum of who they currently are and work, through authenticity and extreme accountability, to create new realities where we can thrive and excel. In short, The Brown Mama Mindset wants to make you the Mama who really can think her way out of her own problems.

We will do this by forming a Brown Mama Mindset based on the principles of authenticity, accountability and, finally, self-mastery. In other words, it's going to be all about yo' mind Mama.

The Brown Mama Mindset does not operate from the perspective that Black mothers are the problems in our families and communities, it works from the perspective that the correct steering of the divine female mind that is in each Brown Mama is the solution to the problems in Black families and communities.

Within each Brown Mama exists a mental steering committee that once fostered in the spirit of self-love, is capable of moving mountains and righting the wrongs of a million errors.

Once you've first developed a mindset of self-mastery, loving yourself, healing your relationships, and rearing and raising children will be simple as you operate from the perspective of internal truth and well-being. You will know what is right for your life once you know what is right for *you*.

As I've worked with Black mothers in the Pittsburgh region for five years I've come to realize that Black moms are struggling in these areas:

- Managing their day-to-day lives
- Building alliances and relationships with men
- Parenting with standards
- Creating and sustaining a productive home life

In those five years, I've seen moms purchase how-to guides, get tons of advice from friends, attend seminars and *continue* to struggle with their problems. What I've realized is that the way Mamas **think** about themselves, their homes and their relationships stops them from making lasting change, not their inability to engage in positive behaviors.

Along this journey, you will complete exercises in the companion Mama Map Workbook that will assist you in practicing and maintaining the mindset mastery that is necessary to embrace your motherhood journey and live your best life.

I suggest that you read 1-2 chapters a week and take time to reflect, journal in your Mama Map or talk to others about what you've read. As you'll learn in Chapter 1, the very first thing you'll need to do to develop this Brown Mama Mindset is to think about time differently. So, don't rush. Mindset shifting is a continual process which takes time.

You won't be done being a mom until you die, so read this book at your own pace.

By the end of this book, you'll be able to answer the question: "What is stopping me from living in my life's purpose?" You'll also have a clear set of Brown Mama Mindset principles that will help you continue to strengthen your new way of thinking.

Consider this book a mental exercise which is building your capacity or challenging you to think about your life. *The Brown Mama Mindset* will invite you to be authentic with yourself about how you really feel about everything from decorating your home to going to church and how you felt the first time you noticed your own insecurity. The companion activity guide, *The Mama Map Workbook*, will help you to reflect on the new feelings and thoughts that will spring up from the well of your soul as you process all this information and make new agreements about how you want to share your new mindset with the world.

With a spirit of invitation, I will ask you to reflect on the current state of mamahood for us Brown Mamas in America, and remember the stories of the Brown Mamas of our past. It's important that we understand where we've come from as Black women in order to evaluate our current circumstances with an eagle's eye view so that we can move forward to dream new dreams for our lives and the lives of our children.

I want you to carry this book with you as a real guide to evaluating how you are experiencing and valuing your motherhood journey year after year.

I want you to pull out this book the day your daughter takes her first steps and the day your son graduates from high school, because you're going to need it. The Brown Mama mindset is not developed overnight, and please know that I am still working to master many of these principles. In the words of one of my girlfriends, "We are in this Mama thing together." This journey will not be easy as we examine how the collective mind of today's modern Black mother has been molded and shaped unknowingly by misinformation and stigma.

But, we MUST do this! We must do this because our children deserve better. We must do this because we deserve to be loved wholly and completely. We must do this because deep down inside of us there is an empty well that just wants to be full again.

So, without further ado, let's get it Mama!

SECTION I: LIFE

Chapter 1

Time Race

"And, time was." -Anansi the Spider

I get déjà vu A LOT. It's something my middle sister and I have in common. On any given day, I'm walking down the street and all of a sudden will realize that the very moment I'm currently experiencing feels familiar, as if I'm remembering it, not living it. I'll realize that I dreamed that exact moment prior to that day. Some people call this crazy talk, others say there is some scientific reason why this happens. I've never delved into the meaning behind déjà vu. I just know that it happens to me all the time.

The Brown Mama Mindset

Although I know everyone doesn't get déjà vu, what I do know is that everyone gets glimpses into their future. Sometimes they come before a life altering event in the form of a whisper, encouraging you to change directions or to stay the course. It may even come in the form of meeting someone who is on the life path you are destined for if you don't change course.

I meet new women all the time in my line of work. As the founder of Brown Mamas, an online and offline national support group for Black mothers, I've learned that you can tell a lot about a woman by the way she is dressed, how she walks, wears her hair and her topic of conversation. I've become so well trained in understanding the idiosyncrasies of Black mothers that I can tell you the age, marital status, income level and anything else a Black mom might put on a job application after one glance at her. Mostly because I can see glimpses of myself in all of the women I meet. I don't just know them, I see them.

A few weeks ago, I had this latter form of déjà vu. I met a young woman whose shoes I'd once walked in. I could see, smell, and feel the life path that was formerly my destiny all over her. I felt sad for her, but

Time Race

I also felt the need to write this first chapter as a way to forewarn other women, like me, who continue (by choice or default) to follow this same road.

It was a beautiful morning in April. The sun was shining and I was beginning to get super excited about gardening season. I got up early and drove to a local dollar store to pick-up gardening gloves for my dig time later that morning.

As I entered the store and was instantly excited because the small garden section was stocked to the nine, like they'd just put all of the garden items on the shelves moments before I walked in. As I optimistically made my way over to the shelves, a Mama called to me,

"Are you the Brown Mama?"

Now I've been told several times that I'm a local celebrity. I've been super reluctant to accept this because I'm a semi-introvert and enjoy a quiet, chill life. I love Beyoncé but have no desire to have her recognition. That's a lot to handle.

Still, I love connecting with my Mamas. Therefore, the hug fest began. I turned around and greeted her with a smile. We exchanged niceties and asked the usual questions about each other's kids and shared that we were excited about the summer time.

Our convo came to an end as she told me she lived near me. As we both entered the checkout line I asked her if she needed a ride. She did.

We ended up talking the entire car ride, or at least she did. I did most of the listening. I asked a lot of questions about where she worked, what she liked to do for fun, how old her son was and how he's doing in school you know those sorts of questions.

I love hearing people tell their stories, so I listened intently and noticed a common theme running through all of her responses. This Mama felt like she was running out of time.

You could hear the mental treadmill she was running in her head in every word detailing her obsession with her future. From hoping her 6-year-old son got into a good college, to her longing for a career in real estate that would help move her family into a bigger house, to her hopes for a newly entered relationship, this was a Mama who's focus on the future was controlling her thoughts at every moment.

Time Race

It was overly evident that life had become a race for her and she'd stopped recognizing the grace of every second a long time ago.

The tick-tock of time was running her life the same way it had run my life years ago. I could tell that her mind was constantly running a 100-meter Olympic race toward the future, even though her life was moving at the same pace everyone else's life moves – slow.

The "time race of life" starts for most of us Mamas right after we have our first child, especially when we are single moms, but regardless of our marital status.

I remember the thoughts that ran through my head when I gave birth to my oldest son. I cried when I held him in the hours after he was born because he was so beautiful, because he was ME, because I knew that what was about to happen between the two of us was divine.

It was as if, even during the pregnancy, I had no idea that I was actually capable of producing another person. After seeing him, I realized that God was real. I was holding living proof of the Creator's power.

The Brown Mama Mindset

After the tears of joy dried and the sentimental thoughts faded, the alarm in my mind went off and the clock started ticking.

The tick-tock of achievement for his sake – or so I told myself. The tick-tock of jobs and bills, and the tick-tock of needing and wanting a father for my son. The tick-tock of trying not to be a teenage, pregnant statistic. And overall, the tick-tock of wanting to prove to my child, and even more so to the world, that I can do this. I wanted to prove that I wasn't one of **them**. It's the time race that is familiar to all Brown Mamas, single or not.

What I sensed on this Mama was that same out-of-breath, rat race, striving for success, all hustle with no flow mindset that I felt after my son was born. It is a feeling of deep insecurity and constant longing. This treadmill mentality took over every inch of my being as I embarked on a quest to hide and run from the feelings of instability that sprung up when I realized that I'd birthed a child in a less than ideal situation.

Instead of trying to live a life of internal fulfillment and wholeness, I began covering up and pushing away this feeling of deep instability by achieving, accomplishing, buying and impressing. Life was no longer about being successful in my own right, but became a race to become the ideal candidate.

I thought to myself that this was important because I had to be a good role model for my son. If he was going to be 'successful,' he'd need to see his mother do it first, right?

I sensed the time race in full activation in the young Mama I met that morning.

Every statement she made, every gesture, every step she took was FULL of unsure contemplation, an inability to accept her current self and a lack of gratitude for who she was becoming.

It's as if she was at the starting line of a track meet and someone fired the gun. She had taken off running with no consideration for her own internal well-being.

Unlike mothers from other cultural groups, we have the distinct disadvantage of starting the race with an already internalized inferiority complex that tells us we will never be good enough. We're not good enough to be good mothers. We're not knowledgeable or intuitive enough to direct our own life path. It's normal for us to live in bad neighborhoods and we are certainly not capable of raising our children, are just a few of the myths we often internalize and, unknowingly, act out in our mom-life.

So, we start. We strive to graduate from college. Put our kids in every activity that we believe will guide them toward a path far from the one we've taken. (Which subconsciously sends them the message that WE are not good enough.) We trust everyone who says they know more than us to have a hand in leading and rearing our kids and directing our lives.

Some of us try on daddies like we're trying on shoes, looking and longing for that man that can help us to do what we believe we are not capable of doing ourselves. While others get so indebted to schools and student loan that once the degree is on the mantel we still can't afford to pay our light bills. Ultimately, we overcompensate for our lack of internal worth by dunking ourselves and kids into the pool of an **assumed** success path.

The Brown Mama Mindset

On the contrary, the way of the Brown Mama Mindset is that of undergoing an internal soul-based self-examination to search for our internal map that will lead us to an understanding of our present circumstance. Developing a Brown Mama Mindset gives life internal meaning that can be expressed authentically in our outward lives.

Rather than running the treadmill of life in hopes that success finds us, we become the Mama Map makers of our own destinies.

Mothers with a Brown Mama Mindset have an inside-out approach to life, knowing that their soul's connection to Source Energy (God) is what will assist them in unlocking the doors to life's greatest answers. Their connection to Source Energy is also what will help them make the right decisions when it comes to rearing and raising their children and engaging in mutually beneficial relationships.

That includes everything from what career path to take to how to best parent our children so that their light shines too.

The Brown Mama Mindset

Mamas with the Brown Mama Mindset understand that the feminine principle of this earth is constantly gifting us with a beautiful female essence called intuition. When we meditate, study, pray and fast we strengthen our intuitive ability to know what is right for our lives and, the answers to life's questions flow from us, **unforced**.

Brown Mama Mindset thinkers understand the power of invitation. We've figured out that all we need to do is **invite** goodness, success, joy, abundance and love into our cosmic space by realizing our own greatness! Those with the Brown Mama Mindset realize that the YOU of right now is the only YOU that is meant to exist at this time.

Rather than focus on being outwardly successful, Brown Mama Mindset thinkers live a life of internal fulfillment that can't help but shine in our exterior lives. Brown Mamas are uniquely blessed this way.

We do this by slowing our lives down to a pace that is manageable and sane. Because those with a Brown Mama Mindset have surrendered future outcomes, realizing that what is most important is that we are currently (at this very moment) working in our purpose. As long as we are leading a life that fulfills our God-given mission, all outcomes will work in our favor.

We choose to think positive thoughts that focus on present living and forgiveness of past wrongdoings of ourselves and others. When you have a Brown Mama Mindset you realize that each moment has a butterfly effect into the future of your life. Therefore, moments should be cherished and not taken for granted.

A mama with the Brown Mama Mindset doesn't mind pushing back a business meeting to cook dinner with her kids. Although her toddler may temporarily leave her mentally and physically exhausted, she sees growth on the horizon as she is constantly adjusting her persona and physical life to accommodate another being. A mom operating in the Brown Mama Mindset realizes that SHE is the mission of her life, and whatever purpose she chooses must help her to transform into the person she needs to be to leave a legacy of female excellence to all who live after her.

A Historic Understanding of Time

Our Ashanti ancestors understood that for African people time was unending, teaching us not to be at odds with time. The quote "Time was," from the critically acclaimed Anansi books comes from the African concept that because we birth children, life is unending for us; for each generation is simply a continuation of the energy and desires of the previous generation.

In short, whatever work the Creator sees fit to leave undone in your life will certainly be continued in the next. For that reason, we should not rush time, run from it, or turn it into an object with which to manipulate and control.

Mothers with a Brown Mama Mindset possess a clear view of what time really is. We understand that no moment is as important as right now. Who you are and where you are at this very moment is exactly who and where you are supposed to be. The past led you to right now. The future is determined by what's happening right now. Right now, is all that matters. When we have the Brown Mama Mindset there is no need for us to run. Walking will do just fine in this moment.

It's okay to slow down. It is righteous to slow down. It is godly to slow down. Let the inner goddess inside of you shine by giving her time to heal and, consequently, glow.

In ancient African cultures, women are often talked about as being the holders of the Kaa. The Kaa being the divine human spirit that was manifested in creation by the Creator. Because we birth Kaa through our wombs, it is understood that we are divine creatures ourselves.

While we are with-child, we hold divinity inside of our bodies. Having gone through this experience, we are exceptionally prepared and have divine insight into what it takes to care for and nurture our unique child. After all, at one time you and your baby shared the same body, blood, spirit and essence.

Well that innate Brown Mama Mindset doesn't cease after you give birth to your child. You are still divinely chosen. Express your unique mothering divinity by stepping into the place the Creator meant for you.

The Brown Mama Mindset

Out of all the on-board tools God could have given us as a creation mechanism, the one thing that was given to all women is a womb. The one thing that women can do that is completely, absolutely impossible for men to do is birth children.

That says something about the importance of motherhood. When a woman gives physical birth, there is an equal spiritual, emotional and mental transformation that takes place. That transformation should not be rushed.

Motherhood is the course. When you rush your day-to-day life with motherhood in the peripheral you are missing out on so many opportunities for internal transformation.

As you struggle through the early years of screaming infants, and stubborn toddlers, the Creator is calling you to become more patient and long-suffering.

The joy you will experience during your child's sweet spot years (ages 6-10) will make you a more loving and compassionate mate for your life partner.

The temperance and keen eye for deceit and manipulation you will develop during your child's teenage years will serve you well in the workplace.

Time Race

And even as your children become adults, you will become a balanced mentor who is able to be in charge without being in control, possessing great restraint.

During each moment of your motherhood journey your mindset is being fortified from the inside out. But you can only gain access to the transformative opportunities of motherhood when you get off the treadmill and live life in the present. Allow yourself the time to grow rather than racing through life chasing carrots that may, or may not, lead you down the right path.

Get out of the time race and start to really live your life moment by moment. Stop trying to force success and focus on being success.

We sometimes get the principle of attraction wrong. You don't attract what you want, you attract what you are.

Got a mission? Great!

But, what good is it to accomplish your mission only to be the one who hasn't benefitted from it? What good is it to become a motivational speaker who can't motivate herself? What good is it to be a life coach who has a screwed-up life? What good is it to be a relationship expert who can't stay in a relationship?

Here's the thing Mama, good kids are the product of good parents. Kids grow into well-rounded and knowledgeable people because those qualities are modeled for them by the adults who raise them.

You've got to decide, right now, at the beginning of this book whether you will stay on the time plantation, or get off the treadmill and start living.

Harriet Tubman said she could have rescued a thousand more slaves if only they knew they were slaves. Are you a slave? Are you a slave to success, materialism, relationships, goals, money, and time? To what degree is that slavery keeping you on the plantation of the world's dream?

Stop saying, "If I had more time." You do have more time. Your time limitations are solely based on your perception of time. Your job takes up all your time because you allow it to. You're constantly shuffling your kids because you've decided to do that. Living a life of internal security is all about spending your time on the experiences that will give you the most life fulfillment (not the most money), and allowing the Universe to do its job of worrying about and providing for tomorrow.

It is time for us Mamas to return to our natural state of well-being: wholeness.

I'll end this first chapter with a scripture: "Therefore I tell you, do not worry about your life, what you will eat or drink; or about your body, what you will wear. Is not life more than food, and the body more than clothes? Look at the birds of the air; they do not sow or reap or store away in barns, and yet your heavenly Father feeds them. Are you not much more valuable than they?" Matthew 6:25-26

Mama Map Invitation

How do you feel about time in this very moment? What is the #1 time sucker in your life? In what ways are you a slave to this time commitment? If you did not have this time constraint, what would you do with your time? Utilize your *Mama Map Workbook* to track your feelings about time each week. This activity will help you decipher how you really feel about time.

Chapter 2

Nourished Roots

"You cannot overestimate the unimportance of practically everything." -Greg Mckeown, Essentialism

I don't care about what I wear in the morning. I'm not sure if this is a result of mothering, being over age 30, or the fact that most days I'm with my kids all day. At some point I just stopped thinking about the clothes I wear every day. I realized some time ago that the thought of 'what I should wear' doesn't occur to me until after I've taken a shower and put lotion on. I only think about my daily attire at the point that I'm about to actually put it on. Some mamas might call this letting yourself go, but I just view it as a way of getting rid of thoughts that are not essential to my life.

This idea of essential living has all but consumed my life lately. I believe deeply in Greg Mckeown's life philosophy of focusing on the essential things of life. I know that the things you value deeply, should guide your daily thoughts, behaviors and actions.

I didn't develop this principle of the Brown Mama Mindset overnight. It took some pretty dire circumstances for me to begin the process of understanding the trivial nature of most of the activities I engage in on a daily basis. One situation in particular started me down the path toward essential living.

About 5 years ago I was inspired. I'd began talking to my biological father, who I'd not known for my entire childhood and most of my 20s. At that time, I'd just given birth to my third son and was in the middle of a deep postpartum depression that derived from what I thought was the unproductiveness of living a life solely based on motherhood. During a long phone conversation, he asked me what I was doing with my life.

Nourished Roots

I responded, "Right now I'm just focusing on trying to be a good mom."

I said it and cringed inside. At the time, I thought that motherhood was hindering me from an assumed success path that I just knew I was destined for.

In response to my singularly focused new lifestyle, my father began to praise me. I was shocked!

He said that it had been a long time since he heard a woman say that. He began to tell me about his own childhood and how instrumental he thought parenting was in uplifting the plight of African-American communities. He told me stories about early African cultures, like the pygmy fathers, who heralded fatherhood as a mainstay of their culture. This immersive view of fatherhood was one of the reasons the pygmy of the Congo had been able to remain a culture intact for tens of thousands of years.

This conversation planted a seed in my soul. I no longer saw my position of mother as irrelevant. I began to see how important it was to be intentional and focus in on motherhood. He woke me up to the fact that I was raising Black boys and they needed me to show them the importance and value of parenting by being there mind, body and soul.

The Brown Mama Mindset

That seed grew into a plant. The plant bloomed flowers and I became a motherhood cherry blossom tree. I was overflowing with the feel-good stuff of mom life.

Fast forward one year and Brown Mamas was birthed. I'd moved back to my hometown of Pittsburgh from Brooklyn, NYC with a message. I was on a one-woman-mission to spread the word on the importance of focus and intention in mothering, specifically for Black mothers. I myself had begun to reap the rewards of my father's advice and was overflowing with joy about it.

I starting telling people through blogging and videos how vital it was that Black mothers develop a new mindset around child-rearing. It wasn't long before this old, but new idea was embraced with excitement. I began receiving grants, being called on to tell my story by local media outlets and garnered a great following of Black mothers who shared my sentiments of focus on motherhood being the key to unlocking the struggles of Black families. I was on cloud nine that my message was so well received.

I took the grant money, buried myself in community missions and projects, answered every call for an interview and even began taking one-on-one lunches with moms who were struggling. All my social media accounts were overrun with mommy-related requests. Some days my phone would not stop ringing with notifications. I'd glance at my cell phone before going to bed and would have 200 Facebook messages and no less than 20 emails to boot. However, it wasn't long before my inspiration turned to resentment.

By now, my children were in daycare (a place I vowed my children would not be). I barely saw my husband, I had no more romance or joy in my personal life. I was back on the treadmill, and this time it wasn't to prove a point. It was of my own doing.

I longed to be in my garden planting flowers with my oldest son. I remember wishing that I'd never told anyone that I was a happy mom because now I had to act like a happy mom even when I was NOT a happy mom.

I was no longer focusing on motherhood. I was entranced in the idea of focusing on motherhood. The idea had taken over. That coupled with my cloudy vision, lack of professional support and cluttered schedule almost killed my inspiration.

I began to resent social media, community organizations, and even the moms who were a part of the Pittsburgh Brown Mamas group. I'd poured so much out of my cup without replenishing it that I began to resent the thought of continuing with the mission I'd once had so much internal motivation for.

But, as us mamas know, the sun is faithful. It always shines, always dawns a new day.

After the breakdown came the breakthrough message that it was time to get back to basics. It was time to get essential. It was time to nurture my roots.

As you'll learn in upcoming chapters, my garden is my God Space. The green around my home holds a special place in my heart not just because of its beauty and peacefulness, but also because it has taught me so many lessons.

One thing all plants have in common is they all have roots. All plants may not have pretty flowers, juicy fruits or even grow in dirt, but EVERY plant has roots. In that same way, every woman has roots too. Your roots are your foundation and they are how your soul extracts the vital nutrients of peace, rest and laughter to grow your life.

If a plant has no roots, it cannot live, let alone thrive. The roots of a plant extract the nutrients from its surroundings in order to give it food (love). Roots are also often buried deeeeep below the surface. I know of some plants that will drill their roots up to 20 feet deep to extract water. (You ever tried snatching out a dandelion root? It's EX-HAUST-ING!)

At that point in my life my roots were shriveled, dry and in need of nurturing and protecting. So, I had to pause to reflect and remember what inspired me in the first place; I recalled long conversations with my mom and dad. I remembered taking my kids to the park every day. I thought about Sunday morning conversations with my husband in bed. I remembered the feeling of dirt between my fingers. These experiences are the nutrients my roots need to allow me to thrive as a woman, mother and loving human being. These things are essential.

The Babies WILL Die First

One of my least favorite houseplants is the Spider plant. While they are well-known for their easy care, I just think they are ugly. They have little tendrils that grow from them when they're taken care of properly. In my house we call them babies. Spider plants grow their babies as long tendrils that extend from the plant with little baby spider plants at the ends.

Formerly, I have not been the best indoor gardener. I often forget to water my hanging spider plant. One of the things I noticed about my spider plant is that when it's not getting enough water or sunlight, the babies began to die before the plant itself begins to wither.

As a mom, I thought that rather than the plant sacrificing its children, it would wither itself. FALSE. One thing nature understands better than we do is that everything flows from a source. When a source begins to wither everything in its shadow will dry up first. When a stream dries up the coast line is barren first. It literally dries up from the outside in. One of the signs of a person suffering with cancer is that their hair falls out. Their heart doesn't stop working first.

It's the same concept with motherhood.

If the Mama (the source) is not practicing self-nourishing activities, the outward signs appear first. Their children may be spending exorbitant amount of times in front of the TV, dinner might consist of cereal and oodles & noodles daily, the house may be messy all the time.

The bottom-line is that when mommy is all dried up, no matter how unintentional, the babies will die first.

When we neglect to care for ourselves we have the misconception that we can continue to care for our children without missing a beat and that everything will be just fine. We seriously think that we can keep the business going, keep the relationship fresh and keep looking good even when we are dying on the inside. That's simply not true. Trust me Mama, your kids notice your absence, your boss is thinking about firing you and your husband knows the lovin' ain't right.

The spider plant personifies what happens to moms when we fail to properly nourish our roots.

But the good news is, unlike the spider plant, we CAN control how much water we get!

Root Recovery

If you don't want to experience the burnout I just described, or need to recover from it, you need to be intentional about maintaining the flow of your essence that means protecting your roots.

So, how do you begin root recovery? You need to begin by asking yourself what is essential for you in maintaining your sanity. Do you start to feel wobbly if you don't visit your mom once a month? Is a healthy diet essential to balancing your thoughts? Is it a consistent prayer life? Is it playing in the back yard with your kids once a week? What activities and behaviors are essential in maintaining your balance?

Once you've identified what nourishes your roots you must bury your roots deep by protecting the behaviors that keep you nourished. You will do this by developing rituals and routines that give your essential behaviors staying power. (We'll talk more about this in Chapter 8: Rituals & Routines)

Nourished Roots

But even before that, you have to develop a dogged mindset about ONLY doing what is most important FIRST. Or as Greg Mckeown puts it in the book *Essentialism* "distinguishing the trivial many from the vital few."

Doing what is most important first, won't' feel good in the beginning. Especially when your mind has been hooked into what it thinks is essential. You will feel the tug and pull to do what everyone else is doing. You will want to run when your roots are telling you to walk. You will want to talk when your intuition says listen.

But Mamas who possess a Brown Mama Mindset understand that if you want to live a life of little regret, of joy and of being rooted in feeling good on the inside so that your very presence is illuminating on the outside, you must learn to do what is essential.

Your intuition will be your guide to essential living. In fact, those essential behaviors we just talked about: BINGO! They will be rooted out by your intuition. Your inner-self will tell you what makes you, YOU.

If you break down the word intuition, you have 'in' and 'tuition.' Your intuition, literally tells you what behaviors, thoughts and interactions pay off for your inner-self and outer-self. It guides you in creating a reservoir of inner self-confidence and energy that can be used in dealing with the circumstances of life.

But, in order to maintain that gorgeous soul, you must protect your inner-self by consistently engaging in those essential behaviors that nourish your roots. Once you've mastered this aspect of the Brown Mama Mindset, you will not only have developed a criteria for guiding life decisions, but you will also be unshakeable. You will have firm and unmoving roots (foundation) for which to build an essentially excellent life.

Mama Map Invitation

Use the illustration to create an Essential List for your life. Begin by writing down what is essential for your sanity in the middle of the diagram and work your way to the outer part of the image going from most important to least important behaviors.

Chapter 3

Stop Losing Your Keys

"Because Jesus has given me the keys to the kingdom my life will never be the same."
-My Aunt Cynthia's voicemail

You can't even begin to understand how many times I lost my keys as a teenager. I can count on more than two hands how many times I'd get all the way home from school and realize I'd left my keys. I'd constantly be waiting for my little sisters at a nearby neighbor's home. Hence, I got to know my neighbors well and during my high school years I formed a close relationship with a wise and patient community elder named Ms. Gaston.

I became a regular at her home because of my constant forgetfulness. I spent many hours sitting on Ms. Gaston's porch or in her living room surrounded by old newspapers chatting about Oprah, God, 'the stories' and our increasingly gentrified neighborhood. It was there that I gained a key that would unlock a very powerful life lesson.

Ms. Gaston was a chubby, brown-skinned old lady. Her home was warm, but full of keepsakes. Just like many of the other elders in our central Pittsburgh neighborhood called the Hill District, she was part of the aged population relegated to the permanent underclass of the sick and shut-in. (You know, one of the names you hear called out every Sunday during the church announcements.) She was not sickly, but she did possess the common elderly denominator of being "unhelped." Most of the elderly in my community were like Ms. Gaston. She rarely had visitors, used public transportation to get from point A to point B and watched A LOT of television. Although these were not ideal living conditions, I think they were conditions ripe for having a close relationship with a stupid teenager like me (and I was soooo stupid).

My relationship with Ms. Gaston was built out of necessity and a kind of teenager fondness built on pity and an inkling that I might need Ms. Gaston later in life. (My inkling was spot on.) Still, most of our meetings were predicated on the fact that I was going to lose my keys and Pittsburgh weather is well-known for dipping below zero degrees in the winter. Most days I'd tried to walk as fast as I could pass her house hoping she didn't see me, but occasionally I'd go sit with Ms. Gaston and listen.

On one such day, when I was inclined to sit for a while, I found myself wrapped up in a conversation about life with Ms. Gaston. It was there that she granted me access to one of my most treasured life lessons.

We sat on her porch looking at the trees that shot-up behind the houses across the street. It was a beautiful summer day, but there was a darkening of the sky and slight breeze on the air that made the leaves whistle and let us know rain was coming soon. As she rubbed her long, dry and slightly wrinkled hands together she began to tell me how she'd come to rely on the rustling of the trees for advice.

My teenage mind should not have been able to interpret what she was saying, but in that moment, I knew exactly what she'd meant. It was like an antenna literally extended from my head and caught the signal that transformed what she was saying into language my young mind could understand.

It was in that moment that she told me whenever I got lost or confused to "listen to the trees." She said that the trees are always speaking. Following the exchange of wisdom, the trees whispered to me that this was a moment I should not forget.

They told me to hold tight to this piece of advice and to remember that Mother Nature had the answers to many of life's questions. They told me that the answers were old and never changed and that it was only the seeker and questions asked that seemed to revolve like the doors at Macy's in Grand Central Station.

That advice has never failed me to-date. Every time I've found myself in a place of bewilderment; when my mind was swirling and my emotions seemed uncontrollable, listening to the trees has helped me pause my thoughts long enough to anchor my spirit and find the answer that I knew all along. The trees have proved a faithful confidant and truth teller.

Ms. Gaston taught me **why** I was always losing my keys. In Ms. Gaston's world, it was revealed to me that key-holders exist in everyone's life. Ms. Gaston was one of the many key holders I've met in my life.

Life's answers, or *keys*, are created by the Creator, Universe, God, (THE *Key-maker*) whatever you want to call the mystic essence that made and continuously expands our world. Our Creator then, creates life as a huge puzzle, placing life's answers, or keys, into the people you interact with and experiences you will engage in. They are your *key-holders*. You are the *key-master* of your life. It is your job to decode your engagement and experiences and master the lessons that our Creator has placed on your life path.

And, you need to know that you are not going to find the keys that the Creator has made for you by staying to yourself. You must find your key-holders.

I had to go into Ms. Gaston's world to retrieve the powerful lesson of Mother Nature that was locked away in an unlikely person. It required discomfort. It required patience. It required me to go outside of myself, and trust that someone other than me knew more about life than I did. Retrieving that key made me keenly aware of the priceless gift of advice from the elders.

How many times have you been just like the teenage version of me? You're standing at the door, right on the cusp of being home and you realize you don't have the key. You have a thought about where you may have left the key, but it doesn't matter because in that moment it's inaccessible.

How many times have you been locked out of life because you lack the substantive qualities to gain access to an experience, opportunity or person? You might meet a really good guy, but because of your lack of depth and inability to see potential, you are unable to receive his love.

Maybe you had a child before you were mentally, emotionally, and spiritually mature, so you're unable to enjoy your motherhood journey, and as a result you're sowing unintended seeds of negativity in your child.

The point is, don't get to the door and not have your keys. Take every opportunity to gain knowledge, understanding and wisdom from those around you that you are gifted. Don't get locked out of the door of your destiny just because you devalue the people and experiences in your life that are trying to teach you.

Mastering the keys to your life is all about realizing you are NOT an island roaming around in the world. Your life is a symbiotic system ebbing and flowing, and dependent upon the moves and countermoves you make with the people you interact with.

Even when you accomplish something great, you will need mental and emotional fortitude to keep you there. This level of personal strength is often gained through the ancient art of listening at the feet of the elders, or those older than you.

If you want to unlock the mysteries of your journey then you must locate the keys to your life that are locked up in the people, NOT things, around you. Many of those keys will be locked up in the people you live with, and in your journey toward getting to know yourself.

Life works this way.

Your life is not only constantly making and revealing keys for you to find and master, your symbiotic life is constantly making and holding the keys to life lessons of each individual you touch.

With each experience a person has, keys are being created, stored and mastered. Dependency is a fact of life.

I know that you've been told that everything you need to succeed is already inside of you, and that's partially true. You possess the insight, skills and intuition necessary to unlock every door that the Creator has for you. You are the key-master of your own life, but you are not a key-maker or key-holder for your life. You will need help on this journey.

While you are ignoring your daughter's request to read just one more book, you may have just missed an opportunity to locate a key. That nagging feeling that your job is not fulfilling your spiritual need is your soul yearning to unlock a door somewhere else. When you and your spouse are in the middle of an argument that the two of you just can't get over, you might also be missing a potential unlocking.

Yes, some of your keys are waiting for you "out there" in the world, but the vast majority of your keys are waiting to be unlocked in your parents, spouse, children and neighbors. Your keys are waiting to be mastered through meditation, journaling, loving and praying. And you know what else I've learned? It's those closest to you and those experiences with which you hold the most disdain for, that have the most intricate and impactful keys to unlock for your life.

For example, the quote that I opened this chapter with is from my Aunt Cynthia's voicemail.

Growing up I can honestly say I didn't value my aunt the way I should have. I am named after her, and consequently have almost the exact same name she has. She was one of the constant people in my life.

However, as an adult I am beginning to see the similarities in our personalities and realizing the life difficulties she must have had to endure in order to become the person she is. My aunt teaches me through our various interactions that when life gives you lemons, you try your best to make lemonade. She teaches me that the flaws you point out in someone else's personality are often the very things that you don't like about yourself. Most importantly, she teaches me to devalue no one, and that EVERYONE you meet understands something that you don't.

For this reason, each time you step foot into your home and community, you must be aware that you are stepping into the Matrix. **You've got to become a decoder.**

Your home and neighborhood is made up of the fundamental chapters of your life. It is the place where you will not only find the keys to life lessons, but it's also the place where you will master and set intention for your newfound treasures. And most importantly, YOU become a key-holder for your children, your spouse, your mama, your daddy, your aunt, your best friend and like Ms. Jackson, for your neighbors.

It is of the utmost importance that we instill the vitality of building community in our children. We need to understand, and help our children understand, that creating physical community is about more than economics.

Building community is about instilling a culture of pride, security, self-knowledge, well-being and overall sovereignty into a group of people. They will be the key-holders of new realities for our people.

The Problem with Losing Keys

I believe the abundance of lost keys in our communities is the reason for the untapped potential, negative mindsets and lack of love that so many of us Brown Mamas live through and see played out in our everyday lives.

During a recording of an episode of the Brown Mama Blueprint Podcast I spoke with a home ownership expert who talked about the direct correlation between teenage violence and home ownership. She stated, and it is true, that according to the U.S. Census Bureau, an increase in homeownership in any U.S. city automatically leads to the same decrease in crime.

We talked about how so many of our brown babies become adults and have no home to come back to. They have no key connection to the communities they've left. Many see this lack of connection between African-Americans and the communities that raise us, as foundational cause of the sweeping gentrification that's currently happening all over the United States.

Many millennial children have grown into adults who do not see their former communities, and the people who dwell in them, as places of love and power. Rather, the 30-somethings of today see their old neighborhoods as places of burden that they must single handedly, many without the necessary skill sets to do so, uplift and empower on their own.

Therefore, these same neighborhoods that were hotspots for unlocking the doors that led to the Black Renaissance, Civil Rights and Black Power Movements have been forgotten by the adults of current time.

Parts of Brooklyn, the D.C. Metro area, Detroit and even my own hometown of Pittsburgh were left dilapidated and crime stricken for years as children of the 60s and 70s abandoned them for the seemingly greener pastures and lawns of the suburbs. This created an entire generation of women and men who see inner-city neighborhoods as places to run away from.

Those same communities are now being infused with millions of dollars in real estate investment.

Stop Losing Your Keys

The massive confusion among our people regarding **where** we locate our life keys has led to a huge loss of potential wealth for Black people.

Just like the young teenage me, so many of us try to run pass Ms. Jackson every day without being seen.

When we prefer our careers over our kids we are running. The consequence: they develop after school programs and college curriculums that place high value on materialism and gaining wealth, and little value on cultural pride, community development and advancing Black interest. Those same children become adults who run away from their communities, thereby continuing the cycle of untapped Black unity.

When we don't visit our parents, we are running. The consequence: an entire industry is developed and gains government funding to neglect our elderly as they die. These same elders once provided our villages with a wealth of knowledge on everything from child rearing to how to effectively engage in the rules of servant leadership.

When we see that overgrown vacant lot in our neighborhood day, after day, after day, after day and we fail to get our lawn mower and take action, we are running. The consequence: the sweeping gentrification you are currently seeing in every major U.S. city in the United States.

Long story short, if you don't take care of your children, home and community someone else will.

What we don't realize is that while we are running, someone else is paying attention. Someone sees all the doors you are not unlocking. While you're failing to remember your keys and unlock your doors, someone is getting a key made, checking it twice and walking through the door of your destiny.

Someone sees how little attention you pay to your kids. Someone sees the arguments you have with your husband every day. Someone sees your neglected community. Just like the investors who came out of the woodwork to stimulate the economies of those neighborhoods we forgot about, somebody is going to unlock your destiny; it just won't be you.

One of my virtual key-holders, Oprah Winfrey, hit me with one of my favorite life lessons when she said, "Energy, like you, has no beginning and no end. It can never be destroyed. It is only ever shifting states."

Energy cannot die. Once a desire springs up in your heart it MUST be fulfilled. In the words of Jesus, "Ask and it is given."

But the thing is, the energy can be fulfilled within your state of matter, or it can shift states and be fulfilled in someone else's state of matter. It doesn't care who fulfills it; as long as it comes to fruition. So, when that desire to buy a home sprang up in your heart; the request was fulfilled the moment you made it. Our Creators is always faithful in honoring righteous request.

However, once you decided that your credit wasn't good enough or it wasn't possible for you to save that much money, that desire realized it couldn't be fulfilled with you. So, it sought out another key-master. It's really that simple.

The keys that you choose to forget about in your children, mates, community and self will be found and mastered, just not by you.

Become a Key-Master

So, what do you do to stop other people from mastering your keys? PAY ATTENTION! Get off the treadmill, start nourishing your roots and put your keys in the ignition and DRIVE!

Talk to your neighbors. Find out your purpose and take action TODAY!

Listen to your children when they talk, when they play, when they tell you something is wrong or right, LISTEN. Your child chose you, when he/she came into your womb. Their spirit literally said, "I want to go there." In that space is the only space I can manifest my unique divine energy. Your child chose YOU! He/she deserves your undivided attention, at least some of the time.

Get outside and get involved in your community. Find out what your purpose is. Why did God see fit to put you in this community, during this time and with the unique set of skills and talents that you possess?

Talk to your neighbors. Find out **why** the God in you is attracted to the same neighborhood that the God in them is attracted to. The problem is that too many of us Mamas really believe in coincidence.

Newsflash Mama: There's no such thing! Ever!

You live where you live for a reason. You are who you are, for a reason. You've got to take on the challenge of locating the keys of your life, so that you can decode and master your life's purpose.

Realize that your eyes, no matter how educated they are, do not see or know all. You are helpless without other people to depend on.

Independence is a false reality that we are socialized into as a result of our own insecurity and egos. Dependency is the true, natural state of all human beings.

Locating the key-holders in your life is all about admitting that you are dependent upon the Creator and that you are a part of the Creation.

In the words of Traci Ellis Ross, the lead actress in Black-ish, "You don't get a life, You ARE a life." The people, not things, around you are creating, molding and connecting you to that life. You are on an adventure with multiple passengers. Now you can either sit in the back seat, or you can put those keys in the ignition, pack your people in the car and go for a ride!

Mama Map Invitation

Find a key. What is the first real life lesson you learned? Who taught it to you? How do you use it in your everyday life now? Next, ask yourself what keys are you holding? How can you contribute those skills and talents to your community? Use the illustrative charts in your *Mama Map Workbook* to map your key-mastering abilities.

Chapter 4

Accept Your Exceptionalism

"It is not until you accept that you are not normal that greatness will occur in you."
-Ragnar Lothbrook, The History Channel's Vikings

I have always been drawn to the number 8. Before I ever picked up a numerology book or learned the science of numbers, I knew that the number 8 figured prominently in whatever my life journey would be. Everything important in my life always happened on a date with the number 8 in it and I'd always feel comfortable about the prospect of success when I knew that the number 8 was somehow involved.

When I decoded my numerology grid, it was of no surprise to me that I was largely defined by number vibration 8. In fact, everyone around me from my children to parents were somehow influenced by the 8 vibration. The powerful, success-driven number 8 has become a definitive characteristic of my life.

The interesting thing about numerology is realizing that personalities really are 'fixed.' The day a human being is born, *they are who they are*. Now adjustments can be made, personalities can be altered, environments can affect who a person is, but at their core they'll always be the same. They'll always be drawn to or turned off by certain people, places, things and behaviors. Even when they succeed at overcoming their desires, the desire exists, no less.

Every day we are bombarded with messages that tell us we need to pinpoint what is wrong with our personalities and begin the process of 'fixing' ourselves. We need to stop being resentful, impatient, unkind, jealous, etc. We need to dive deep, and really dig out those 'negative' emotions.

The Brown Mama Mindset rebukes this idea.

Accept Your Exceptionalism

None of us are Beyoncé. Beyoncé ain't even Beyoncé. In other words, we are all flawed. We don't wake up perfect, or even good. We wake up with crust in our eyes, bad hairdos and smelly breath. But, isn't that how you are supposed to wake up?

Surely, common sense tells us that everyone wakes up to the imperfections that are so perfectly innate to humanity. So, why do so many of us shy away from being seen in our natural state?

It's because we've convinced ourselves not to accept what is natural. We've told ourselves a stream of lies that say an 'ideal' person, situation, lifestyle or culture really does exist. When in reality everyone wakes up ugly.

Everyone in this world has things they hate about themselves. Everyone has parts of their body that they wish would disappear. Everyone has an inner critic that is constantly pushing its own agenda toward 'perfection'. Even among the upper echelon of our society exists a group of people who project an outward aura of perfection and happiness *only* because they've been able to suppress their ugly so deep. But, we still see their ugly in the overall craziness of the world that rears its horrifying head on the news every night.

But, the beauty of ugly is that it also has a pretty counterpart. Just as everyone wakes up ugly, everyone is equally capable of something great.

This is the approach to self-help that the Brown Mama Mindset encourages. In order for you to see the greatness in you, you must first accept ALL of you! Once you've accepted all of you, you must then proclaim that you are, quite simply, the BEST YOU that you could possibly be.

In the work I do with organizing and supporting Black moms, I'm always surprised at how willing Black mothers are to accept 2nd place in the mothering category. I once asked some of my Mamas whether they felt comfortable saying that Black moms are the Best moms.

Most of them said absolutely not. They said that all moms are good moms, and that they weren't sure that any mom was capable of being the best mom.

But, I think many of them missed the point. Proclaiming you are the best mom is not about superiority as much as it is about giving yourself the

Accept Your Exceptionalism

inner-confidence necessary to overcome any obstacle that is presented.

And boy do Brown Mamas have a ton of obstacles to climb over.

Every morning when I rise I say to myself "Muffy Mendoza is the best mom there is." This helps me to overcome the mom guilt that sinks in for so many Mamas as we move throughout the day. We feel guilty about going to work, guilty about having girl's night, guilty about buying ourselves a new shirt.

Many times, this mom guilt comes from our inability to pat ourselves on the back at the end of each day. It creeps up on us because we haven't fortified our inner domestic diva by replaying the good of our motherhood journeys, rather than the bad.

Despite the fact that Brown mamas throughout history have an exceptional heritage of queendom, high intellect, overcoming crazy odds and even mothering the children of our enslavers, we still refuse to believe in our own excellence.

This will not do Mama! In order to begin adopting and implementing the Brown Mama Mindset, you must start accepting your own exceptionalism.

Mothers with the Brown Mama Mindset know that they are capable of unprecedented excellence. This new mentality, not only propels them toward overcoming obstacles, but demands self-mastery.

Once you've implemented and maintained your Brown Mama Mindset, accomplishing career goals, rearing well-rounded children and staying in functional, loving relationships becomes an extension of the perfectly, flawed excellence that you've mastered within.

Flawless Philosophy

Some of the greatest musicians and athletes have claimed flawlessness and have been praised due to their announcement of superiority.

Muhammad Ali is best known for his over-confidence. He's probably better known for saying "I'm pretty," than for his boxing style. When Beyoncé declared herself "Flawless" millions of fans flocked to the statement. They branded their t-shirts, hats and even coffee mugs with the words "Flawless" in attempts to convince themselves that they too believed in the perfection within.

Accept Your Exceptionalism

And, Beyoncé's husband, Sean Carter (better known as Jay-Z) has declared himself a "god to the game" since his multiple platinum Blueprint records. By using the abbreviated HOVA (a shortened version of the Latin term Jehovah which is used to describe the Hebrew God) as his lyrical nickname, Jay-Z has all but elevated himself to the true embodiment of hip-hop royalty just by speaking it into existence. Tina Turner (simply the best), Remi Ma (I'm conceited, I got a reason) and countless others have uplifted their internal self-conscious and external reputation as flawless just by saying it.

It takes a ton of gusto and the removal of a lot of internal waste to declare unequivocally that you are the best at something. So, when I say Brown mamas are the best mamas it is not out of an inability to spot flaws. I say this with full sight and right knowledge and because I want you to see in yourself what I've already seen in myself.

I don't know that any mother in the history of our planet has endured the hardships that have been bestowed upon the backs of Black mothers. The passing down of the plight of single motherhood from generation to generation that many of us have lived through is in and of itself a troubled experience.

The onslaught of sexual abuse and mistreatment that has lurked in the shadows of Black mothers since our arrival on American shores. The distress of working 9 to 9 while attempting to raise children we barely see, would drive any woman insane.

Black women have built up a resistance and resilience to these types of systemic deprivation that has never been expressed in humanity itself. Despite low-income households, many Black mothers still send their sons and daughters to college AND manage to start their own businesses.

In lieu of insufficient time, we still manage to take care of our children and family members with a vigor and sweetness that turns grown men into boys when they utter the words "Mama." There is no figure more prominent, revered or loved in America than Black mothers.

Yet and still, WE don't see ourselves that way. Many of us don't see ourselves at all. It was the infamous Ragnar Lothbrook, the leader of the Germanic Vikings, who said during the History channel show also titled by that name," It is only

Accept Your Exceptionalism

when you accept that you are not normal that greatness will occur in you".

I once heard a local minister say that self-acceptance equals empowerment. So, the trouble with Black mothers' inability to accept their exceptionalism does not lie in our lack of power. (For we are more powerful than even we know). It lies in our inability to **accept** ourselves as powerful (filled with power).

I've often run into mothers who have this idea of "bad Black mothers" embedded in their souls. We all know these mothers. They are the mothers, just like us, who are unable to accept compliments for their children. Every time their kid is given a compliment they counter that encouragement with a negative characteristic about their kid. These are the mothers who always want more for their children. They buy their kids the Jordans, then the True Religion Jeans, then the brand new car at 16. It's as if they are trying to prove something or fill a void opened by their own insecurity. These are the mothers that cringe inside if someone even mentions that Black mothers are the best at anything. Because to them, all moms are good moms.

The Brown Mama Mindset

You'll have no argument from me there. Surely every mother loves her children and cares for them as best she can.

But, not every mom faces the dilemma of raising a son in violent neighborhoods with anxious cops. Not every mom is forced to send her daughter to school knowing there is a greater chance she will be sexually or physically abused, might not make it home or is more likely to face the systemic poverty that chases women that look like her. Not every mom is forced into a dating pool where half the men are in jail, gay or are just plain ole 'can't get rights.' (OKAY!)

You are not a run of the mill mama, YOU ARE EXCEPTIONAL. You are exceptional because, except by the grace of God NO ONE could, and can endure, what you have.

Our divine Creator did not place you at the dawn of humanity while still upholding and keeping you during the hells of slavery only to ascend you once again to the astute platforms held by First Lady Michelle Obama or the nation's FIRST woman millionaire, Madame CJ Walker in order for you to be normal. No! You are far from normal, YOU are the

Accept Your Exceptionalism

standard and embodiment of all female energy on this Earth!

Use your naysayers as motivation. The multitudes will remind us of our place at the bottom. They will try to keep the ghettos, crack babies and baby mamas at the front of our minds. But, let us use that as motivation. And for every crack baby, let's us remember that there are more of our Black daughters enrolled in college than any other race in America, according to their Census Bureau. For every baby mama out there, 52 percent of Black women are married. (Yeah, they just tell us about the 48 percent of us who are single and forget about the rest of us.) For every nay there is a yeah! Every electron has a proton, and every time you fall, you will rise again. Do you know why? Because You are the BEST!

Being the best does not mean you are not flawed. Being the best doesn't mean you have dinner on the table everyday by 5, or that your kid makes straight A's. Being the best simply means that you made it. That you have accepted the power you have over your own life. It means you acknowledge that you are in possession, in this very moment, of everything necessary to be who you are purposed to be.

Accept it mama! You are not normal. You are so far from normal that the mundane hardships the average mom has to endure are like cartwheels for you!

The first book in the Bible commands us to take dominion of this earth. Accept your exceptionalism and take dominion of what has been laid before you. You are a daughter of God, be that!

Everyday remind yourself how far you've come. Remind yourself of God's grace and accept the power of divine female, motherly energy that exists uniquely inside of you.

Now, let's get you on that path to realizing the EXCELLENCE God put ONLY inside of you!

Mama Map Invitation

Your assignment is to create a Brown Mama Mantra to empower you on your motherhood journey. Use the illustration in your *Mama Map Workbook* to create an affirming "I am" statement that will remind of you're the exceptional qualities you possess as a Black mother.

Chapter 5

Joy Reservoir

"I don't put a lot of stock in happiness, because it's based on happenstance. For me, that means it can change as things change. I have a healthy level of contentment, and a well of joy I can dip into during rough times."
-Diamonte Walker, one of the best moms I know

Getting married while you're 6 months pregnant on the hottest day of June will not make you happy. I remember my wedding day like it was one hour ago, mainly because I've never been that hot before. I wore a heavily sequined halter top gown that was supposed to be cinched at the waist, but instead just sat on top of my protruding belly like a hot, heavy, white comforter. The train that strolled nearly 1 foot behind me wowed my wedding guests, but for me it felt like I was dragging a basket of laundry that was tied to the uncinched section of my wedding dress.

Just the thought of that dress and the ridiculous way it fit my pre-labor body makes me cringe on the inside. By the time the wedding got underway, I'd stripped out of my sequined nightmare of a dress to pee at least 3 times in a tiny bathroom stall.

Then there was the makeup. While 3 tons of makeup caked to your face makes your wedding photos look flawless, it does nothing to help the internal flame that exists inside of a woman in her third trimester of pregnancy who's carrying a load of sequined laundry like it's a halter top. The makeup artist had literally glued a set of tarantula-like, false eyelashes to my thin almost unnoticeable existing lashes, and every time I blinked I felt the weight of a million pigeon feathers on my eyelids.

As if the 100-pound dress and pigeon feather eyelashes were not enough, I was hungry; fiercely hungry. A person knows no hunger until they are 6-months pregnant and forced to attend a reception where 25 people want to give a congratulatory speech to the bride and groom before the food is served. I had nothing to eat except cookies and water to quench my hunger until 2 hours into the reception.

Then there were the doubts. While I'd known my husband for almost a decade prior to our nuptials, something inside of me couldn't stop wondering whether I was doing the right thing or not. And, it showed.

My wedding vows sucked. While I mumbled at the altar about simple love and how my husband and I simply needed each other's love, or something cliché like that, my hubby-to-be gave the most eloquent story about our first meeting and went on to lovingly and poignantly describe his love for me. In comparison, I'm sure no one remembers the words I said. I don't even really remember, I was too busy sweating and hoping we'd soon be able to retreat from the outdoor pergola to the air-conditioned reception hall.

My husband's family are among the kindest people I've ever met; still I know they were hoping their son married a Caribbean girl, or at least a New Yorker who's cultural and social ways were closer to their own. Me? I was an outspoken, dominant, immature mid-western/east coast Pittsburgh girl who, as my mother would say, didn't know her butt from a whole in the wall. At the moment of our I do's I'd just began to realize that every action has a consequence, and I hardly had any basic principles for living my own life. I was young and just as simple-minded as the vows I'd spoken that day. I was just a girl.

I can't say that I was happy on my wedding day. More than anything I was tired. I was anxious, fearful, unsure of the future, hot and hungry.

Even though I could remember my wedding day as a time of physical torture, I have so much joy in my heart when I think about that day.

My Brown Mama Mindset helps me to remember the things that were so overwhelmingly joyous about that day. I distinctly remember walking out of my 2-story housing project unit in a beautiful white gown, greeted by a flood of sunlight and a little brown girl who asked "Are you a princess?"

I responded, "No, I'm getting married and you will one day too."

That moment alone expands my **joy reservoir** with the thought that this young caramel colored girl

Joy Reservoir

may not have known anything about marriage until I walked out of my unit wearing that heavy, white sequined dress. Looking back on that day, I think the dress wasn't for me at all. It was for her.

The smile on my son's face the entire day of the wedding is a joy reservoir so large it could sustain my thirst for decades.

While I was exhausted from the day's events and anxiously fearful of the days ahead, my oldest son's then 6-year-old face had joy written all over it. He was so excited to finally have a man to call dad. He was ecstatic about having all of his family in one place to celebrate his new family. Thinking back on that day, our uniting as husband and wife wasn't just about us becoming one, it was about breaking a generational curse of fatherlessness that had existed in my family for the last three generations.

Then there was my husband, who for some odd reason was so happy to marry me. Every time I looked over at him he was crying tears of joy or smiling ear-to-ear. His joy was so contagious that I smile ear-to-ear 10 years later at the thought of his expression. While I may not have been the girl his parents wanted back in 2008, I've definitely grown into the woman he needs now. His unconditional love has molded me into a kind, patient, still outspoken, but only necessarily dominant woman that he enjoys growing old with.

That's what finding your joy reservoir is all about. **Finding your joy reservoir is all about slowing down long enough to remember the things that nourish your roots,** instead of dwelling on the things that may not have delighted your senses.

Happiness is fleeting. Rather than seeking happiness, Mamas would do well to develop a Brown Mama Mindset that allows them to be mindful of the meaningful life experiences that provide immense amounts of constantly accessible joy.

Having joy doesn't mean you won't feel sad. Being sad is an acceptable life experience. Everyone experiences grief, sadness and mundane contentment at some point in their lives. However, those with a Brown Mama Mindset know that joy is on the horizon.

Those with the Brown Mama Mindset understand that these emotions are a part of life and should not be rushed away or hushed. Rather, they should be fully experienced and allowed to run their course with the inner-standing that their joy reservoir is constantly available when they are ready to readjust to a more cheerful mindset.

Mothers with the Brown Mama Mindset possess a joy reservoir that allows them to see the cup as neither half empty nor half full, but as refillable. They understand that the contents of their life cup will constantly fluctuate, but that when they are ready, filling their cup is as easy as going to the tap and turning on the joy reservoir.

Simply put, it's about remembering the good instead of remembering the bad.

Optimism is the Daughter of Joy

Most times joy does not seem like a realistic expectation for us Brown Mamas. Many of us are constantly bombarded by downtrodden neighborhoods, adversarial relationships and interactions, and financial breakdowns that hardly feel humane, let alone joyous.

Knowing this, many will ask, "How can I possibly find joy in my life?" I can think of one culturally-relevant simile that accurately describes where joy is found in lives similar to ours.

"Joy and pain are like sunshine and rain...they're both one in the same." -Frankie Beverly & Maze

Joy is in the recollection of your breakdowns and acknowledgement of the growth and grace of your breakthroughs. Yes, us Mamas go through many breakdowns in life from untapped potential to even the violent loss of our Brown Babies.

But, what we must do is realize that there is so much potential for joy, even in loss. That potential is called optimism. In simplest terms optimism is one's ability to look on the bright side.

In more tangible terms, optimism means reaching for your next, most accessible, positive emotion.

Rather than dwelling on a negative occurrence, mothers with a Brown Mama Mindset will locate the silver lining of their trial and reach for an emotion that is more positive, even if only slightly more than the one they are currently experiencing. She understands that just like any other emotion, there are varying degrees of joyfulness.

Joy Reservoir

For example, if I am currently sad, my next, most accessible positive emotion might be numbness. While numbness is a far cry from joy, at least at this point I've removed sadness.

Next, I might move from numbness to resentment. Then resentment might turn to melancholy, Melancholy might turn to contentment, and so on and so on.

While we might not be able to immediately access feelings of joy, optimism is the driving force that helps us to continually reach for emotions that move us beyond the negative mindset of our present.

We cannot allow our environment and previous mindsets to convince us that depression, sadness, anxiety and other low-vibration emotions are permanent. This prevents our minds from returning to their natural state of wellness, which is joy.

The point is to incrementally move from disagreeable mindsets and emotions to ones that are agreeable with living your life's purpose; because so much of becoming the person you are meant to be is about maintaining a healthy level of optimism.

It's all about falling in love with the process of becoming great; ups, downs and all that's in between. That will require optimism.

Brown Mamas will do well to be grateful for, and optimistic about the trials we face, as we are being refined in the fire. Other mothers might cave under the pressure we face on a daily basis.

An old African proverb says, "A child who is carried on the back will not know how far the journey is."

The joy of the journey is only made accessible to those who walk it. We are blessed because we walk the road. Rather than taking our trials for granted, or being ashamed of them, we should recognize these experiences for the true optimism and joy inspirations they are.

Joy: Returning to Your Natural State of Wellness

Everything you've ever wanted is waiting on the other side of your decision to consistently choose joy. Joy is your natural state of well-being, but it is only constantly accessible to you once you realize that it *is* your natural state.

Joy Reservoir

As I mentioned previously, I recently developed a deep love of studying numerology. The basis for numerology is the understanding that everything and person on this Earth has a vibration.

Most of us learned about the 3 states of matter in school. Well this is the basis for understanding numerology. A solid vibration is so attracted to itself that its movement is condensed, tight and almost unmoving. Water vibrations are still attracted to each other, but move more freely around each other, allowing it to be shaped and molded to whatever its container demands. A gas vibration has no attraction at all and prefers to move freely and almost sporadically in some gasses, with no containment at all.

Mamas seeking a Brown Mama Mindset would do well to think of their emotions and desires as holding a vibration just like the three states of matter.

Quoting my father, and the teachers who taught him, "Every thought has weight, shape, color and form". Every emotion, thought and action you engage in everyday emits an energy in the form of a vibration.

Joy being among the highest vibrational energies accessible to us humans is an attractor of desires. When you reach the point in your life where you can consistently maintain a state of joy, the things you desire will be attracted to you, effortlessly.

This is because your desires need to be received by an optimal growth vessel where they can manifest.

As we discussed in Chapter 3: Stop Losing Your Keys, when you want something if you're vibrational pull differs from the thing you desire, that desire has no problem finding another vessel that it can manifest itself in. Every success or assumed failure in your life is indicative of previous thoughts and behaviors that have pulled those outcomes toward you.

For example, think about how you felt when you finally got your baby to sleep through the night. It likely required a consistent routine (or set of behaviors), mindset and emotions. Those consistent energies practiced over a period of time led to your baby reciprocating the very vibrations you were emitting.

Your desires are just like that baby. They need YOU to be ready. Once you've provided the optimal growth environment for your desires, they have no problem allowing you to manifest. It's really that simple.

On the other side of a consistent joyous mindset lies your effortless ability to be the mother, wife, friend, career woman, entrepreneur or whatever that you want.

You must do this by constantly following and using your instincts and intuition. Simply do the things that bring you joy, and don't do the things that don't bring you joy.

When it's difficult to be joyous, cherish your breakdowns, remember your breakthroughs, and dip into your joy reservoir often.

And when it gets really hard to reach for joy, remember that the hot, heavy, sequined, white dress might not be for you at all.

Mama Map Invitation

This week we are going to use our *Mama Map Workbook* to keep track of our emotions. Utilize the illustrations provide to rate your emotions each day.

SECTION II: HOME

Chapter 6

Be Pretty

"Being pretty is fun."
-Tamika Sumpter as First Lady Michelle Obama

I remember the first time I realized that being pretty has intrinsic value in the way it makes me feel. In the 6th grade I made a new friend. She was to be my best friend for the next decade of my life.

My mother didn't allow me to go to many friends' homes as a teenager, but after she met Aunt Dee, my best friend's mom, she was at ease and allowed me to go visit as often as I wanted. I was excited to have a best friend and be able to get away from my mother's strict, but righteous, rules.

The first day we pulled up to Aunt Dee's house I knew there was something different about her style.

She had a small garden in the front of her house that was surrounded by tall hedges. Rocks shaped like frogs dotted the small space between her plants. I've never been a fan of animal adornments. Hens, frogs, fish; any of these decorations in a house disturb me, but Aunt Dee managed to arrange these green frog garden stones in a way that gave them style and grace. Something I'd never seen done before.

On the rare occasion that someone had a decorated yard in my neighborhood it tended to consist of bright fake flowers, and cheaply made signs that, while welcoming, didn't have much stylistic aesthetic.

One breezy spring day when we walked into her pathway, I could hear the enchanting sound of wind chimes and the smell of fresh, airy cinnamon delighted my senses when I walked into her decorative storm door.

As I entered her home, I was overtaken by freshness. The light scent of laundry blowing in the breeze on a summer day greeted my nostrils upon entry. I was also welcomed by a colorful Aztec print vase which sat atop the first landing of the staircase. The vase was complimented with cattails, wooden reeds, earthy tones of red on feathers and plants, topped with yellow and green sprouting out from its circular opening.

Then came the warmth. Her home was simple, but pleasant and full of character. The mahogany wood furniture that adorned the living room felt like it played jazz music even when there was none. The sturdy almost antique furnishings seemed to hug the huge bay windows that allowed the perfect view of their quiet city street.

Her kitchen reminded me of an old-school New York city-style apartment. She put teas in special chalk-black tin containers and kept just enough food in her fridge to feed herself, husband and my new best friend.

And, her home matched her style. Aunt Debbie possessed an understated Africanesque flamboyance that I'd never encountered before. She knew how to pair jeans, an ethnic piece of jewelry, bohemian sandals and her signature Caesar haircut as if she was a Nigerian model walking the streets of Paris.

Everything about her style was quaint, chic, ethnic, and pretty. After meeting her, I knew that I wanted my form of pretty to be just like hers when I grew up.

Up until that point in my life, the only version of pretty I'd ever known was my mother, who reminded me in her youth of Halle Berry. While my mother's girl-next-door form of pretty was constantly complemented on by my friends, and even my boyfriends, I knew my mom's style wasn't *my style*.

Now, as a 36-year-old woman, I know what pretty means to me. My attraction to Aunt Dee's style had more to do with the way I felt in her presence, then the way she looked. The essence of her physical style matched the vibrational level of spirit and emotion I wanted to feel. Aunt Dee was my own personal style icon.

That is the importance of pretty. Being pretty is NOT about stuff. Let's be clear.

Being pretty is about meeting the vibrational level of your desires. Just like prayer and meditation, what you look at, and look like each day creates feelings, thoughts and actions that play themselves out in your day-to-day life.

Just like the Aztec, warm-colored vase that greeted me when I first walked into Aunt Dee's house, I've always wanted to have depth of soul, and warmth of spirit as a part of my persona. The physicality of that vase aligned perfectly with the essence of feelings, emotions and mentality that my inner-being was seeking.

As we develop our Brown Mama Mindset it is so important that we remember EVERYTHING physical has an equal mental, emotional and spiritual vibration.

Our favorite pair of earrings are our favorite because we like the way they look, yes. But, that pull toward them is also very closely aligned with the way they make us feel.

Think about how many times you've changed or added to your personal style. What did that change signal in your life? Why did you change it? How did that change affect how you felt? Did that style switch-up change the way people perceived you?

Changing, adapting or even staying in line with your personal style is all about manifesting your inner desires, thoughts and emotions on the outside.

When you're wearing your favorite pair of jeans, you have a sway in your hips that you do not possess on the days when you have to wear those pants that don't flatter your figure.

Brown Mamas deserve to feel good, not just about the way we feel on the inside, but about the way we look on the outside. As we develop our Brown Mama Mindset, we should also be exciting our senses by allowing them to manifest on the outside.

Simply put, have fun with your pretty!

Buy some new earrings. Go to the second-hand store and collect some $1 shirts or shoes you can experiment with. Mama, EXPRESS YA SELF!

Along this journey you will have ups and downs. You will find there are things about yourself that you like and things about yourself you don't like. As you are having these AHA moments, be easy with yourself. This means letting the agreements you've decided to break, or keep along this journey manifest themselves on the inside, *and* the outside.

As you allow this outward transformation to take place, you will feel drawn toward mastering your own personal esthetic. As you make new personal agreements and let go of others, you may decide to let your hair grow long or finally make the big chop. The color purple may become your new accent color or you may decide that polka dots are the best. It's up to you.

We enjoy our day more when we look good, feel good and are surrounded by pretty things because it assists our spirits in reaching a level of positivity and receptiveness where we are more likely to manifest the desires of our hearts.

Your Unique Feminine Fingerprint

My mother and I went to the movies to see the President Obama and First Lady love story, *South Side with You*. It was too cute. I loved seeing our first Black President swoon his woman in such a romantic and thoughtful way.

My favorite part of the movie came when First Lady Michelle Obama was getting herself together prior to their date. She was doing what most of us sistahs do. Checking her figure in the mirror, putting on lipstick and smoothing her edges...lol. When her mother asked her who she was getting all dolled up for, she responded in the sassy way that most Black women do, saying that Barry was no one special, but that she tried to look her best whenever she went out and that **"being pretty is fun."**

That spoke to me.

I'd been saying for years that Black women NEED a pop of pretty in their lives. Most of us are yearning for it and don't even know it. The First Lady confirmed what we've always known, but just didn't want to hear. Being pretty is fun, and us sistahs love doing it.

Have you ever seen one of our sistahs from "the hood" sporting bamboo earrings, fitted jeans, a satin bomber jacket and skittles-colored Nikes like she's walking the couture runway? I have, and I know you can't tell that sistah nothing, weave down to her booty and all. Some call it ghetto fabulous, I call it concrete rose pretty.

In this way, Black women tend to express their pretty very uniquely when compared to women of other ethnicities. Whether city or country, rich or poor, light skin or dark skin, short or tall or any other superficial difference, Black women add a sprinkle of melanin, a soulful expression, a feminine swagger to every element of their life that oozes something one can only describe as Black Girl Magic.

Need some examples? Easy. You can't even compare Christina Aguilera, Britney Spears or any other pop star in white American history to the popularity, style and influence of Beyonce. Next, take your pick of any ancient African queen. From Queen Tiye to Nefertiti, Nzinga, Hatshepsut and the list goes on and on. Queendom never looked so good. Angela Davis and Pam Grier sporting afros puts everybody on notice that the movement is here. Disco didn't even exist until Donna Summers and Diana Ross got a hold of it with their silk jumpsuits, long legs and never-ending soulful, but brisk voices. No matter how chubby Oprah was, she was (and is) the queen of daytime talk. No matter how loud and offensive the voices of racism and sexism of America get, this country knows one thing for sure: it ain't cool, it ain't stylish and it ain't on trend unless WE do it first!

For this reason, mothers with a Brown Mama Mindset would do well to begin to embrace the unique form of beauty African-American women have been blessed with.

Among women, all ethnicities have their own way of expressing their pretty. Japanese women have the traditional Geisha wear, white women have Fashion Week and Parisian fashion as guiding lights for their pretty inspiration, Latina and South American women wear clothing inspired by the flow and brightness of their Samba and Meringue music. What inspires Black women in fashion?

What is our unique feminine fingerprint the product of? Mothers with a Brown Mama Mindset would do well to examine this question with intention and intensity. Black women certainly have our own distinct form of beauty.

From the silk jumpsuits of the disco era, afros of the 60s and 70s and the fly-girl, Hip-Hop inspired loud style of the 80s and 90s, our culture has shaped the fashion consciousness of America.

Mamas with a Brown Mama Mindset will utilize the Black fashion icons of yesteryears as a starting point for deciding how we want to contribute not only to our own wardrobes and style, but also to the closets of the girls yet to come.

Let us remember that what we wear, and what the women of the future generations will wear, is not only about style and being on trend, but is a physical manifestation of the collective thought process during that period of time.

We millennial women, who are in this moment determining the unique feminine fingerprint of our time, must take this responsibility seriously because it is one of the lens we will be viewed through when our time on Earth has waned.

For this reason, it pains me to see a Brown Mama who have given up on their femininity. It is as if she has lost her soul key. In the instant a Black woman forgets her pretty power, she cuts off the chain that has been so particularly passed down to her from the effeminate goddesses of her past.

She loses the spark that is so indigenous and unique to Black women. It is in our DNA to be pretty. When we force this part of ourselves to go deep and lie dormant we miss out on our power and relinquish our own queendom.

Your version of pretty is your unique feminine fingerprint. It is within you on a cellular level. It was passed down to you from your mother, who re-interpreted it from your grandmother, who also re-purposed and renewed your great grandmother's pretty perspective, and so on and so on. Now it's your time to let that lady light shine.

What will it look like?

Mama Map Invitation

I love this invitation. We are going to have some pretty fun. Use your *Mama Map Workbook* to find your unique feminine fingerprint.

Chapter 7

The Little Things

"Gimme some Stevie. Gimme some Donnie. Gimme my daddy. Gimme my mommy. Pour me some sweet tea, spoonful of honey... I don't need no Hollywood..." -India Arie

I have always loved those lyrics sung by the incomparable India Arie. They've always felt like they were just for me. I feel at home in those lyrics with the understanding that life is not about one thing in particular, but it is more so made up of a ton of people, circumstances, places and so on, and so on.

One weekend my mom came over to help me paint my living room. We had girl talk, spilled paint, gossiped and spilled more paint. It was fun. I realized in that moment that home for me would always be wherever I could feel her spirit. It also made me realize all of the moments with her that have made my life dramatic, loving, hard, easy and every other emotion in between. Those emotions are more a part of me than any 'thing' I've ever purchased or been given.

For that reason, I'm constantly looking for signs of her in my home. The way everything in my kitchen is red; from the pots and pans to the dish drain. Why are they red, you ask? Because my mom says that everything in your kitchen should match and I believe her. But, it's not just the red drain and pots and pans that make my home feel good. It's also the little spaces in my home that tell a story or remind me so perfectly of an experience I've had with her. It's the little things.

Focus on creating those type of spaces in your home. Oftentimes we focus so much on buying new stuff for our home and completing big projects in our home that we forget what the essence of home is all about. Home is about having a space that brings you solace, comforts you when life is hard and provides respite when the journey has ended.

Material things are not capable of giving us the deepness of those feelings. But, they are capable of sparking imagination and memory. Those are the kinds of things we should be interested in decorating our homes with.

Items that spark a memory, create an intention and that bring joy when we recollect how we obtained them, are what keeps our minds sharp as we enter old age. They are what fuels us to stay the course. When we become collectors, not hoarders, of sentimental items that bring definition to our story, we create a home that is full of life.

For example, I remember being at Goodwill on a sunny afternoon in May. I was looking for items to decorate our new home we'd just moved into the previous fall. Everything in this house made me excited. The mahogany wood walls, the outdoor brick oven with its cottage style chimney and the original wood flooring made me feel so excited and overwhelmed about decorating.

That day at the second-hand store I spotted this medium sized, golden sun knick-knack. I love anything that reminds me of the outdoors. Home decor that's reminiscent of being in the forest on a warm day automatically catches my eye. I took the little golden sun to the counter, paid $2.50 for it and carried it home.

It looked just right on one of the shelves that extends across the block glass window above my living room sofa. It perfectly accents two, small forest green vases that I'd also found that day. Together they made me smile.

A few months later my sons were playing with their football in the house. You already know how that ended. The golden sun fell off the shelf, rolled down the sofa and hit the hardwood floors. My two younger sons said "Sorry mom," and stood still because they knew that shit was about to hit the fan. I yelled and gave them all the cue to get the hell out of my living room.

But my older son saw the dismay on my face and knew that the little sun held a special place in my heart. He carefully picked up all the tiny pieces and reassured me that it could be fixed. I loved the gesture, but didn't think much of it. The decorating diva in me was crushed.

The Little Things

Much to my surprise, an hour later he emerged with my now-crackled, globe-like sun accent piece. He'd put it back together using tape and superglue.

I couldn't throw it out. He'd worked too hard.

And I actually found that if I sat the sun knick-knack in a very exact position on the glass shelf, you couldn't tell it was cracked. The tape had also created a much sturdier foundation for my little sun circle to sit on. He'd fixed it and made it topple-proof.

That happened two years ago. I still have it. Every time I think about throwing that little golden globe away I'm reminded that my children love me. I remember that at least one of them hates to see me hurt and is willing to spend his time repairing my broken heart when necessary. This little thing holds meaning for me. It gives me hope and fills my home with more than stuff. It fills my home with love.

Sure, I really liked the sun globe, but now I love it, because I love him. I remember his face that day every time I look at it, and I remember my mended heart.

A home is made up of all the small movements you've made over your lifetime, not shopping trips.

That vase you spotted a thousand feet away while at the flea market on one random Saturday afternoon out with your sisters, the sofa table that you "inherited" when the funniest co-worker you've ever met moved out of town, the houseplant that your ex-boyfriend left at your house and you just can't seem to get rid of; those are the items that will keep your memories fresh and your home full of life as you grow old in it.

Your home should be dotted with the footprints of your life journey the same way small islands dot the ocean; revealing big islands as their rocks trickle out to sea. Your home should be comprised of the little things that narrate your autobiography.

So much of that will be determined by the interactions you have with your family. From trophies from your kid's baseball game to pictures of family vacations and items left to you by loved ones who entered the next realm.

I remember when I first laid eyes on my great grandmother's stout, ivory-colored Africanesque bookends. My grandmother asked me to store some of her items in my basement. When she pulled out those bookends, my heart skipped a beat. My eyes narrowed in on them and I quickly said "Can I have those?" They looked soooo me. They belonged to my

The Little Things

great-grandmother Gettings, and it was as if she had thought of me, in particular, when she brought them. They are now among my prized possessions. No piece of furniture from Pier One could ever compete with the way I feel when I look at them. They give me joy!

Now I have a story to tell my children about those sturdy little bookends. I placed them right next to my great-grandmother's picture on my ancestor mantel. My boys likely take them for granted because they've been with us so long, but when they get older one of them will inherit these new family jewels. They will inherit not only a physical object but a story, a period of time and a piece of themselves.

I feel the same way when I walk into my living room and reminisce on painting it with my mom, or when I pass by my little golden globe.

The little things in your home should give you a reservoir of joy that will follow you to any place you call home. The little things should also give your housemates, family members and visitors a sense of where you've been, how you interpret life, who you are and who you're becoming.

Rather than focusing on remodeling your kitchen or buying more picture frames, FIRST focus on getting more of YOU in your home. What is your journey? Who have you taken the journey with? What is your most compelling life story to date? Got the answer? THAT is what your home should look like.

No Rent-A-Center, Levin Furniture, or Ashley Home Store in the world can recreate your personal life story. That's your job. For this mission, we will need a healthy dose of intuition, sprinkled with a little bit of being in the right place at the right time and a big heap of family love.

You will not make your home feel warm overnight. But, what I can promise is that if you take your time. If you keep your home clean, inviting, loving and peaceful, the items that make your house feel good will be drawn to you. Simply put, you attract what you are, and the same goes for your home. The more of your inviting aura, or positive spiritual presence that exists in your living space, the more it will feel like a home you have lived in and loved.

Rushing to fill your home with more things, will turn your home into a house and make it feel like a lobby. You know when you go to the doctor's office and you walk in. Nothing makes you feel like you want to stay. Everything makes you feel **not** at home.

The Little Things

When I initially moved into my house, I was chomping at the bit to add my own flavor to my new dwelling. Every time I'd visit a store, I'd pick something up. If it had trees on it, was made of wood or had even a hint of my favorite warm colors, it hooked me in. Cost was irrelevant. (Something that pissed off my husband, but I was willing to live with those consequences.)

It wasn't long before my house looked good. It had my favorite colors, cute little pictures and all the *stuff* that I thought made a happy home. There was just one problem. It didn't feel good and it didn't look like me. The rugs I'd picked out didn't have a story behind them. The toss pillows I'd found on lonely shopping trips didn't recall memories.

Though I had shopped 'til I dropped and liked each piece I'd purchased, the items didn't have feelings attached to them.

Decorating your home from the "more, more, more" mindset, will leave your home looking like a museum and feeling like a waiting room. You would have spent the money, took the time to decorate and you may even like your stuff, but you won't feel *your* stuff. So, what are you rushing for? You've got plenty of time.

My dad always tells me that it takes 20 years to create a home that you really feel comfortable in. That's because it takes at least 20 years to really experience the fullness of one life chapter. The older I get the more I understand this. It's not enough to fill your home with stuff. Stuff doesn't have memories. Stuff doesn't evoke emotions. Stuff is just stuff.

A House is not a Home

"Do you have a home?"

Anthony had no idea what a home was. The question even echoed in my own mind when I asked him and realized I knew the answer to the question, and he did not. It'd been a decade since I'd last seen Anthony. He'd been my boyfriend throughout my late teens and early 20's. We'd both moved on in life since the last time we talked. We'd both gotten married, become parents and moved from our old neighborhoods. Anthony always had a sadness in his eyes. There'd always been a part of his soul that was broken and you could see it in his eyes then and now.

The Little Things

He responded, "Yeah. I got a big house and a pool. I live with someone too." His response let me know that he didn't have a home, but more importantly that even as a man of almost 40-years-old, he still had no idea what a home was.

Anthony was one of the street kids in our neighborhood. He'd been a drug dealer since he was a young teenager. His mother was one of the sweetest souls I'd ever encountered. But, their family was one of those families that was constantly enduring trauma. From the violent deaths of friends and family members to the loss of close ones to disease and illness, by the time Anthony and I reached our mid-twenties he was the only surviving member of his family.

As a youngster, I'm sure he'd been surrounded by family members who loved him, but as he grew older his home grew colder and colder with the loss of soul, after soul, after soul. Anthony's story teaches us a valuable lesson about what it really means to build a home.

In the words of the legendary vocalist and writer Luther Vandross, *"A house is not a home when there's no one there to hold ya tight and no one there you can kiss goodnight."*

Just as much as building a home is about putting meaningful things that narrate your life story there, it's also about the love that is created under its roof. You are not meant to live alone. You turn your house into a home by loving its inhabitants and creating memories that can later serve as additions to your joy reservoir during hard times that will certainly come.

Building a home is about leaving a legacy of a meaningful life to your children. It's so easy to decorate a house, but it takes more than shopping trips to create a home that your grown children will want to return to.

In my grandmother's words, "People go where the getting is good." Is the getting good in your home? Do you make homemade meals? Does your family spend time reading, talking and building together? Do you celebrate one another in your home? Do you make space for family members and loved ones in your home? Is the getting good at your house?

I can't help but think how much less tumultuous Anthony's life might have been had one family member decided that the getting would be good at their house. This means creating a space where children feel wanted, loved, protected and cherished. That means ensuring that at your home there is a space where loved ones can come for good conversation, a hot meal and homebrewed lessons.

Building a home that is made of the good old-fashioned little things, is about creating a safe haven that insulates its inhabitants from the harshness of the outside world and that, through shared knowledge, provides an authentic template for dealing with the world's realities.

In a home, no question is a dumb one. In a home, no decision stops you from being loved. In a home, everybody gets a trophy. In a home, everyone's true self is safe to show and shine.

In essence, in a home, a golden globe knick-knack can be broken and then put right back together.

Mama Map Invitation

This invitation will invite you to create a little thing that you can remember as you grow old in your home, wherever it may be. Use your *Mama Map Workbook* to give your home a little change with a big reward.

The Brown Mama Mindset

Chapter 8

Make it Smell Good

"Mom! I'm hungry"
-Said by EVERY kid, EVERYwhere

When it comes to making your home smell good, Febreze ain't got nothin' on food. I've walked into many sistah's houses not feeling hungry at all, that is, until the smell of greens or baked chicken hit my nostrils. There's something about the smell of hot food in a warm house on a cold day that makes everything feel warm and fuzzy.

Simply put, good food makes a house a home.

The Brown Mama Mindset

I remember the first time I made something really good. It was the first Thanksgiving after I'd returned from a 4-year stint living in New York City. While living in the Big Apple, my Trinidadian mother-in-law taught me how to do something extraordinary with chicken: stew it.

Brown stew chicken is popular in most Caribbean households. It is made by the searing of chicken over burnt brown sugar and garlic until a rich dark color, and deep savory flavor are achieved. It is an African, turned Island tradition. (And it would behoove all Mamas to learn how to do it.)

Regardless of how widespread this tradition is, I'd never heard of stewed chicken before. (Don't laugh at me mama). One year of living with my husband changed that. The first time I made stewed chicken it was a greasy, unseasoned mess, but by about the 20th time, I finally caught on. I was excited to debut my newfound dish to my family back in Pittsburgh during the holiday season.

The night before Thanksgiving, I seasoned 15 lbs. of chicken to perfection. I added fresh green season (a chopped mixture of fresh herbs that my mother-in-law had also taught me to create), a homemade jerk

Make it Smell Good

sauce, a few cups of orange juice and a bit of olive oil. My chicken marinated for 10 hours. In the morning, I stewed ½ of the chicken in a big cast iron pot and baked the other half. The result: my uncle, who is the chef of my family, said "Muffy I think this is the best thing you've ever made." I was soooo happy! No one else knew it, but my insides were jumping like I was one of those Asian kids at a Michael Jackson concert (RIP).

There's something special about seeing your whole family demolish a meal you've made. Between the ummms, smacking lips and forks clinking and clamoring to the next side dish on their plate, my heart skips a beat. I become a proud Brown Mama. I've fulfilled all the "Mom! I'm hungry" request and there's just nothing like it. Having my uncle's taste buds approve of Muffy's Brown Stewed Chicken inspired me to cook more. Now I can make tasty chicken-chili bean soup, a mean cornbread, taco pie, and my stew chicken is still the talk of the town! Yes, indeed, food makes a house a home.

Making your home a beacon for healthy, hearty meals will make you a fixture in your family's history. Nobody will ever make (you fill in the blank) like you make it. Your name will be remembered for generations to come. Just like your grandmother is likely remembered for making the best peach cobbler, potato salad or candied yams.

There is something that happens to a Black woman's soul when she masters an art that has been lauded as the way to a man's heart for generations upon generations. She joins the club. She earns her ancestral place among the so-called Aunt Jemima's and Big Mamas who literally slaved over stoves to make big meals in the "big house" while still finding energy and the diligence of hand to provide meager leftovers to feed her loved ones. For Brown Mamas, cooking isn't just about full bellies, it's about keeping a legacy of caring for our own alive, even when it seems impossible.

Even after surviving the food desert of slavery, African mothers were able to create an abundance of delightful foods that would sustain our families through Jim Crow and the Civil Rights Movement. It wasn't our enslavement that stole our taste buds and kitchen savvy from us.

Fast-forward 100 years later and many of us Brown Mamas feel defeated and overwhelmed when

Make it Smell Good

our feet hit the kitchen floor. I've talked to countless Mamas who've said they just don't know what to cook for their families. Most say they're not sure what healthy, hearty meals for their families should look like.

They're caught in the conundrum of whether to eat meat, or go meatless. They're confused about how to properly shop for groceries; should they primarily be in the produce section, or are boxed, processed foods just fine? It seems so many of us Mamas have lost our kitchen swag.

As we climbed the corporate ladders, sent our kids to private schools and brought more Louis Vuitton somewhere along the way us Brown Mamas have lost our hip sway.

The hip sway is the movement Black women often make when we are hands-deep in the kitchen firing those burners up. I myself never noticed the swaying of the hips that goes along with even the slightest movements us Mamas make in the kitchen until my dad pointed it out to me. Then it was as clear as day. There is a circular hip movement that most Black women make when we are stirring cake batter, whipping eggs and even washing dishes. It's unintentional, but it is a body signal that tells you that a Sistah is about to put her foot in some food.

Think about it. You're whipping those eggs, and what are your hips doing? They are moving to the same rhythm as your hands are. You stand in the front of the fridge and what happens to your hips? They move in the same direction as the fridge; as if to ask the same question that's in your mind. For Brown Mamas, our hips are more than a body part. Our hips are expressive and they often manifest what is happening in our minds and hearts.

But, when many of us put our homes in the rearview mirrors of our lives, we lose our hip sway and our ability to burn. Now, there are a few mamas who still possess this quintessential way to a man's heart, and you will rarely, if ever, find her single. But, some of us need a road back to our roots in order to remember, with both our hands and hips, the hip-swaying, food mastery of our mamas and grandmamas.

How do we get there?

Just like everything else, we have to start at the beginning. Order some cookbooks, ask for some recipes, go to some restaurants and find out what you like. Find out what your family likes.

More than anything, start where you are. Use what you have. Do what you can. (As Arthur Ashe once said.)

The craziest thing happens just about every 4 weeks in my house. It's usually around the time my kids have eaten all the food and everyone is complaining there is no food in the house. I become a master chef. There is something about necessity that forces us Mamas to become food masters.

In fact, some of the world's best cuisine and master chefs create recipes inspired by what some consider 'primitive' cultures, villages and tribes that have managed to feed their families decade after decade with very little resources.

Some of the last decade's best-selling cookbooks, like the Whole 30, Eat Like a Wild Man and The Pioneer Woman, are all based on the idea that less is more and that there's literally nothing new under the sun when it comes to food.

In other words, there's no need to re-invent the wheel, just sprinkle a little melanin on it. You can start your journey by visiting Amazon and buying the cheapest cookbooks in the category you're searching for.

Just like I did with the Brown Stew Chicken, find a simple recipe and master it. Once your family is tired of that, find one more. Because my husband is Caribbean, I started by locating African and Caribbean inspired cookbooks for $5 or less on Amazon. Or, just go to the library.

There ain't a library in the world that doesn't have a cookbook. All you gotta do is follow the directions.

So, what are you waiting for? Join the club.

Chemist in the Kitchen

Have you ever wondered why the word kitchen is not called the "kitchen room"? Every other room has the word 'room' on the end of it. Living room, dining room, bedroom and so on, and so on. Except kitchen.

Well that's because those 'rooms' where not actually built into homes until much later in human history. The kitchen was the first room. It turns out that the word kitchen first appeared in the English language around 1000 B.C., according to the Oxford Dictionary, while separate living spaces to perform other acts (like sleeping or dining) weren't regular cultural patterns in European culture until around the early 1500s.

Until then, homes in Western cultures had two purposes: cooking and sleeping.

Cooking is important. Even when humans didn't have a room to dine in, sleep in or go to the bathroom in, they've made sure they had a room to cook in. That's because food is medicine for the body and nourishment for the soul.

In the words of African-American activist Shahrazad Ali, "A woman determines life or death for her family every time she steps foot in a kitchen."

When a woman puts hand to pot she can, knowingly or unknowingly, cause heart disease, infertility, diabetes and even death with every heap of salt, dollop of dairy and helping of red meat.

It's not enough that we cook foods that delights the senses, but we must also fill our home with fuel foods that propel our husbands, children and family members toward a nutrient-rich, healthy lifestyle.

Mastering the science of homegrown herbs and spices, making our kitchens vibrant with fresh fruits and vegetables and learning the art of plating a meal, are some of the skillsets that should be at the forefront of our home front goals.

It doesn't matter how pretty or warm your home is if you are killing its inhabitants from the inside out.

For every culinary reaction that occurs in your kitchen there is an equal chemical and physical reaction that occurs in the bodies of those who eat your food (that includes you).

I learned this lesson while homeschooling my teenager during his sophomore year. I found a curriculum that centered on teaching chemistry through the science of cooking.

In the course we learned about all the different kinds of sugar. We learned how sugar manufacturers remove all of the nutrients from sugar cane to form granulated sugar. The book *Culinary Reactions* broke down how some sugars are more complex molecules and therefore, are harder for our bodies to digest than the sugars it gains from fruits, vegetables and other whole foods.

We also learned about the dangers of dairy products, and how cow's milk is purposed for a baby cow to grow into a 1500-pound cow. For that reason, it contains way too much sugar, cholesterol and fat to be fed to a human child who won't even average half its weight as a grown adult.

I could write a book on the information that Chemistry curriculum opened my eyes to, from the original intent of salt as a preserver of foods coming from afar to the use of beetles from South America to make food coloring.

During that school year I realized that cooking isn't just about food, it really is a science. It is a science that cooks must master if we are truly to be the caregivers for our families.

Every boxed, canned and processed food we purchase is filled with excess sugars and salts. Every greasy fast food that slips pass your front door onto your kid's plates is a heart attack just waiting to happen.

Now, I love a good chicken sandwich from Chick-fil-a just like any other mama, but absence makes the heart stay healthy. Most fast food corporations will tell you that their food is to be consumed in moderation, and balanced with a healthy lifestyle.

Furthermore, the kitchen has never been an easier domain to master. From crockpots to toaster ovens and rice cookers, it's easier than ever to feed your kids whole foods in the same amount of time it takes to make a trip to McDonald's.

Cookbooks on 30-minute meals, freeze n' dump recipes and cook-ahead dishes line the bookcases of every bookstore and Amazon.

Food needn't be made from scratch to do the job of feeding your children good, wholesome, homemade food. While so many of our grandmothers, aunts and uncles left behind legacies of warm, comfort food, they also left behind generational curses of diabetes, breast and prostate cancer, heart conditions and other food borne illnesses.

Many of our 'Big Mamas' lacked the information and access to good foods that we often take for granted. It's time that we begin to build a new legacy of love for wholesome foods. It's time that we filled the shoes of the late 'Big Mamas' of our families, but this time adding the pops of color from fresh peppers and homegrown cabbage. We need to do what they couldn't do to make our homes, families and communities whole again.

Whole foods make whole people who can create whole legacies for future generations.

Make it Smell Good

Mama Map Invitation

It's time to burn Mama! You are about to make your first ever WMD (Well Made Dinner). Use your *Mama Map Workbook* to document your recipe using the illustration.

Chapter 9

God Space

"She was an adventurer at heart. But oh how she loved drinking this tea, in this chair, from this mug. Oh, how she loved to be at home." -Unknown

A pop of pink set everything off. I locked the back door, and began walking to my car and there it was, right at the bottom of my patio steps in the garden bed.

POP!

It was the most beautiful thing I'd ever seen.

Then, I looked over to the side of the yard.

POP! POP! POP!

Although I'd spent the entire weekend before planting all the flowers I'd purchased, I had no idea that those little mounds of green would transform into bright pops of pink petunias with the ability to mentally transported me from *my garden* to a botanical wonderland.

It felt so good to walk out of *my* door and be greeted by scents and sights I'd previously only experienced at the zoo, or some other wildlife field trip.

I was straight giddy.

It was in that moment that I became addicted. Every bit of spare time I had that summer I spent in my garden. If I wasn't planting seeds, I was watering plants. If I wasn't watering plants, I was weeding. Once I figured out that all I had to do was place a seed in the ground, and shower down water and love in order for a beautiful pop of color to dot all the barren spots in my yard, no one had to ask me to do landscaping. Rather, I became an eager, voluntary expert gardener.

I was a creator in my own right.

On top of that, gardening made me feel good and allowed my mind a space to wander and create with no pressure or force. The human creator in me made a divine connection with the Most High when I went into Black girl garden mode.

Beautiful. That's the only way I can describe being in my God Space. My garden is the place where life just flows for me. When I'm planting a flower, vegetable or bush it seems my brain is firing off on all channels without the slightest bit of force. With no tug, pull or even concentration on thought, the most gorgeous contemplations envelope my mind and are allowed to take root.

For me, gardening is like listening to my favorite song in heavy rotation or hearing one of those church sermons where you know the pastor is talking directly to you. When my hands are wrist deep in the dirt and the sun is beaming down on top of my hunched over back, God speaks.

The Creator speaks to me in every hole I dig and every plant I water. And not in an abstract way. It's as if the god in me has a direct line to the Creator that can only be accessed when I'm in my garden. That's why I call it my God Space.

Every Mama needs a God Space in her home. She needs a space where she is master. She needs a space where the God on high will come down to recognize her dominance and flow with her in the beauty of Creation.

That space can be anywhere. If you are an avid reader, that space can be in your office. If you can burn with the best of them, your God Space might be the kitchen. If you can entertain and host like a celebrity, your dining room may be your space to express your inner goddess.

And when you find your God Space, trust me, everyone will get put on notice.

The first summer I began gardening, my corner of the busy street I lived on became a local attraction. People would stop at my corner and say how beautiful my garden was. Some would yell out their cars as they rode down my busy street, "I love your sunflowers!"

I loved the compliments, but to be honest, I knew my garden was EVERYTHING. Not because I had the best marigolds on the block, or could grow the tallest corn, but because when I was in that garden it was as if I was the lead of my very own orchestra. My internal brilliance shined so bright that even I was blinded by its glare.

God Space

That's how you know when you've found your God Space. Others will see it, but more importantly, it will build your inner confidence. You will become the sugar, honey, ice tea of your household and you'll know it.

Gardening opened up bragging rights I never even knew were in me. Every time something bloomed I was posting on Facebook. I swear I was more proud of those ripe tomatoes, bright green bell peppers and blooming begonias than I was of my babies when they were born.

Allowing your inner domestic diva to roar is a woman's way of letting the world know that she 'takes care of hers.'

This is extremely important for Brown Mamas because so many of us feel defeated at home. After working 9 to 5, going to school, fighting with fathers and trying to clean up the mess our children have created, it is hard to feel anything, but defeated.

I felt that way prior to getting married. Before marrying my husband and moving to NYC, I lived in a housing project in my childhood neighborhood with my oldest son. My life was crowded. Most days all I did was take my son to daycare, go to school, go to work, come home to do homework, feed the kid, go to bed, then repeat the routine the very next day.

I never noticed the little God Space that sat outside of my house.

Leaving and entering my apartment I must have passed those garden beds at least one thousand times in the six years I lived there.

No one ever told me I couldn't plant anything there. It was actually sectioned off into little garden beds and my neighbor occasionally placed some plastic flowers in her garden beds during the holidays.

Recently, I began to reflect on that little dirt space right outside of my apartment door. I wondered why it had never dawned on me after 6 years of living there that right in front of my house there was a space where I could work toward self-mastery and develop the inner confidence to live the successful life I'd yearned for.

Then it dawned on me, I never knew I had the option. For moms who are running the treadmill of life, the option of creating a God Space seems so trivial and irrelevant to meeting their goals.

Back then my life was so cluttered that I really believed the only relief available to me was at the end of the tunnel of the assumed success path I was on. I thought if I just became the *ideal candidate* by graduating from college, getting the *right* job and impressing the *right* people, I would be happy eventually.

I had no idea that working in my God Space could lead to inner confidence that would propel me toward self-mastery and the life that I was seeking. I had no idea that internal-mastery included having the confidence to live a joyous life just like the one I was creating in my garden.

Those with a Brown Mama Mindset understand that it's self-mastery, not degrees, more money or jobs that activate God's divine presence in our lives.

Simply put, mastering our homes is a way of making the god to God connection. It's a way of tapping into the divine Essence that is our Creator and siphoning off a portion of that magic to activate your life path.

Through the repeated action (or ritual) of planting, watering, loving; planting, watering, loving' planting, watering, loving,'; I was unknowingly activating a spirit of mastery in my own life.

A God Space will do that for you.

Through those actions I was unknowingly planting my own seeds of intention in the Universe that were being watered and loved. By being a good steward of the Earth and my family, I was inviting the Universe to participate with me in self-development.

So often when we think of intention, development and success we think of what we can *force* the Universe to do on our behalf. We pray with a plan already in our heads instead of remembering that outcomes are irrelevant and that the only relevance is the essence (substance) of your intentions.

By this I mean, the essence with which you live your life is what will determine the outcome. If you live as a good steward of that which you have already been given dominion over the outcome will **always** turn out in your favor.

For this reason, mothers who have a Brown Mama Mindset understand that we have been given dominion over our homes, children and communities. It is our responsibility and birthright to master those spaces thereby building a sturdy and righteous foundation for the female generations that will follow.

Once we accept our divine feminine birthright, it behooves us to master our God Spaces by engraining our unique feminine fingerprint into our homes and communities.

We master our God Spaces by growing the best tomatoes, creating and maintaining family traditions, keeping clean and tidy homes, cooking healthy and wholesome meals, supporting and upholding husband-wife relationships and becoming the stewards of righteous and honest family interaction in our communities.

God Space mastery fine tunes the cultural legacy we leave for our daughters and sons. It creates cultural walls that protect our children from Western normalcies like materialism, greed and promiscuity.

Most of all, it makes Brown Mamas the bomb.

Because everybody gets put on notice that when Mama gets home, this house ceases to be a wood frame with windows and doors, it transforms into a God Space.

The Brown Mama Mindset

Master Your Foundation

The last job I had before becoming an entrepreneur was the easiest job I've ever had. Or should I say, I made it the easiest job I've ever had. I was an audio journalist for the former American Urban Radio Networks, which was formerly the only Black-owned radio network in the nation.

I was responsible for making the news sound good. I edited audio, produced shows for newscasters and voiced, edited and produced my own reports. I worked there for 3 years, and after one year I'd mastered the job. My part-time gig that was supposed to take me 5 hours to complete took me 2 hours tops.

Initially, I used the extra time to begin producing my own reports because we were paid extra for them. With so much ample time on my hands, during some months I'd produce over 45 reports extra. My initial goal was to do one every day, but 2-3 days a week I'd produce no less than 3.

Eventually our news director asked me to slow down, as my part-time job was turning into full-time pay for them. I'd mastered my job.

Once I could no longer work on increasing my paycheck there, I started thinking of other things I could do to expand my career goals and financial prospects. I started blogging. After I'd finish my required work, I'd watch Good Morning America, the Today Show and The View. I would listen to their daily chats and wait for them to talk about anything dealing with motherhood. Then, I write an article about it. My blog went viral 4 times in that year.

Mastering the foundational responsibilities of being a mom looks a lot like being able to turn your 5 hour part time job into a 2 hour part time job so that you can build your own empire on the side.

How many hours a day do you spend on managing your foundation every week? By that I mean, how many hours do you spend cooking, managing your time, planning meals, cleaning and organizing your home? I bet it's a lot.

But it doesn't have to be that way. Rather than continuing to spend so much time devoted to the mundane task of surviving, mamas would do well to develop a Brown Mama Mindset of mastering the foundational aspects of life.

We do this by becoming the domestic goddesses of our homes one God Space at a time.

The reason why my job as an audio jockey got so easy was because I did it every day for one year. Every day it was the same repetitive behavior over and over again. Eventually, I could do it with my eyes closed.

We need to begin to think about the foundational responsibilities of our lives in this same way. Your God Space should begin as one place in your home, but over time the mindset of repetition and mastery should carry over to other spaces in your home too.

Those with the Brown Mama Mindset do not believe they can only master one thing.

We do believe in the disciplined pursuit of less because we are truly only capable of mastering one thing at a time. However, once we've mastered one foundational responsibility, like cooking, we can utilize the same mindset and learned behaviors to replicate the same mastery in, let's say, the area of organizing and cleaning.

Work from a position of enthusiasm and start by mastering the thing you enjoy first. If you love gardening like me, start there. If you love cooking, become a master meal planner and chef. Then, you can utilize the confidence you built in that God Space to move on to the business of mastering another God Space.

Your home is the foundation of your life. You will not go very far if you don't master your responsibilities there first.

I've tried to skip this step so many times and it simply does not work. I am a great writer, but writing while dinner still needs to be cooked and the kids are knocking on the door every 5 minutes to say "I'm hungry," kills my writing flow and mom guilt slides in the back door. It's all downhill from there.

You can't skip over the foundation Mamas. It's like building a house roof first. If you don't have a solid foundation on your house, it makes no sense to build a front door, paint or install windows.

But still, it is possible to have a house with no foundation. They're called mobile homes. They can be taken wherever you want them to go. Some of them are even really nice looking, but the minute bad weather shows up, they are literally blown to pieces.

So many of us Mamas have built our lives just like mobile homes. We have no God Space in our homes so we haven't mastered much there. We blow like the wind through life, wearing so many hats that we wake up each day feeling overwhelmed and fickle-minded. Some of us have mobile lifestyles that look gorgeous on the outside, but lack the foundational substance that makes us feel good on the inside. Therefore, when the storms of life come, our emotions, thoughts, and lives wash away.

The care of our homes remains in our peripheral vision while we hop on the treadmill of life and chase an assumed success life path.

But it doesn't have to be this way Mama. Developing a Brown Mama Mindset means putting first things first. It means recognizing that your entire home is a God Space landscape waiting for you to master it in order that you might live your best life.

Living with a Brown Mama Mindset means you've mastered the science of surviving so that you can move on to the art of thriving.

Look at your entire home as a God Space that you will master one space at a time.

God Space

She Loved To Be Home

It took me a while to get there, but I seriously love being at home. I used to be like the Mama we talked about in the first chapter. I used to run to and fro just trying to be away from home, but the more I worked on transforming my home into a place that looked, felt and just screamed ME, it was easy for me to want to be here.

Summers in my garden are the best. Bob Marley, tasty, cold drinks (as my husband would say) and the smell of my gold Day Lilies is just ill (90s slang for awesome, great, grand). But, winters are just as good. Blankets in the living room for movie night, snow days throwing snowballs at the kids, even slugging through the snow to bring groceries into the house onto a wet slippery floor and into the house turns into a memory to be cherished when you learn to love your God Space.

Regardless of the weather, irrelevant of the season, immune to the parties or gatherings that are happening outside, I LOVE MY HOME.

The end-game result of mastering your God Space is to be able to utter those words. You won't say it because you have the most expensive furniture. You shouldn't say or think these words because you live in a good school district.

The love of home shouldn't be born out of materialism or status, loving your God Space should be born out of the intentions you've spawned inside the walls of your home and the karmic love that has returned to you twofold there.

Your God Space should be your God Space because it has quenched the thirst of travel when there was none to be had, because it has provided respite for those needy of love in your life, because you have mastered yourself under its roof.

Giving into the creation of not just a home, but a God Space will make life so much more delightful for you Mama. Most of us spend an exorbitant amount of time in our homes. It would do us well to begin making them places where we are able to consistently access our divinity. It would make us so much more joyous to begin expressing that divinity by letting our inner domestic diva shine.

Instead of being a Mama who runs away from home, be a Mama who runs home to her God Space.

Mama Map Invitation

Find your first God Space. Use your *Mama Map Workbook* to find ask yourself a series of questions that will allow you to locate your God Space within your home and begin the journey toward homelife mastery.

Chapter 10

Routine & Ritual

"The difference between routine and ritual is the difference between having power and being powerful." -Muffy Mendoza

It was never a problem for me and my sisters to clean the house on Sunday. Every other day of the week, my sisters and I hated cleaning the house. We'd argue about it. We would try to erase our names from the chore sheet and print each other's names instead. We'd even come home later than usual expecting that someone else might be assigned our chore. Anything to get out of doing chores on Monday, Tuesday, Wednesday, Thursday, and every day, except Sunday.

On Sundays, cleaning the house was an experience. You always knew when it was time for a deep clean. We'd wake up in the morning and music would be playing softly. By 10:30 am Toni Braxton would be wailing so loud you could hear her two blocks from the house.

Vacuums would be running, Mirrors would be misted and ready for wipe down. All the couch cushions would be on the floor and we would use that long, grey vacuum attachment to find last week's homework and $2 worth of pennies, dimes and nickels. We'd all be sangin'. My mom played so much Whitney Houston and Toni Braxton when I was a kid that I can recite all of their songs just like the pledge of allegiance.

After the cleaning was done, the house would smell good. My mom would be whipping something together in the kitchen, and the next thing you know we'd all be sitting around the TV watching something on The Lifetime Movie Network while munching.

Those were some of the most memorable days of my life.

I know this was a routine for my mom, but it was magic to me. I often wonder if she knew she was creating a ritual. To this day, I do the same thing on Sundays. I wake up and get my coffee ready. I might sit for an hour and talk on the phone, or converse via email.

Then, almost like magic, I'll get up and start cleaning. My favorite Pandora station, which includes the music of Lauryn Hill, Erica Badu and Jill Scott to name a few, starts playing softly and before you know it, that music is so loud you can hear it at the park two blocks away from my house.

The kids start sorting the laundry and cleaning their rooms. Hubby has lost all hope of getting an early start on Sunday football watching and starts hammering something or painting something.

On Sunday's my house is filled with the same feelings of cooperative productivity, teamwork, a shared love for the rhythmic music of our culture and just love.

The generational routine begins again, except this time I know that I'm engaging in a ritual.

When I know it is 'one of those Sundays,' I light incense. I'm sure to dust off the mantel where I keep the pictures of my ancestors who have crossed over and I say a prayer to the Lord that the ritual that began in my mother would come to fruition continually in my sons, granddaughters, grandsons and their children; so on, and so on.

I use the Sunday morning experience that I inherited from my mother to begin a ritual of setting in motion the behaviors that I'd love to pass down to the mothers and fathers that will come after me.

Rather than leaving the passing down of this Sunday morning ritual to chance, I set intention behind it that will ensure it becomes engrained in the spirit world in order that it might manifest in the physical.

I do this by taking all the pictures I want hung up and putting them in their spots on Tuesday. Then on Thursday, I take the screwdriver and screws out of my husband's toolbox and set them out in the spot next to the picture. On Sunday morning, all I've got to do is make a sandwich and put it next to the screws. Once Bob Marley is playing and hubby feels good about the routine of putting the picture up, now it's much easier to get him engaged in the ritual of mastering our God Space.

See, the difference between a routine and a ritual is that a ritual is planned and implemented with a consciousness of spirit behind it. I want my family to feel good about mastering our God Space. I want them to feel so good about it that they willingly pass it down to my grandchildren because they look upon this particular routine with so much enthusiasm.

I suspect my mother wouldn't have had so much of a problem getting us to clean the house the other days of the week had she turned her routine into a ritual that we were enthusiastic to partake part in.

The difference between routine and ritual is the difference between having power and being powerful. Everyone has power. Everyone can be successful. Everyone has the potential to express themselves in a great way. But, only a few people are actually powerful.

Being full of power (powerful) indicates that you've engaged in powerful behaviors consistently and in an intentional and meaningful way, that's ritual. Those powerful behaviors have created a rippling of positive and forceful vibrations through your life that break down barriers of self-doubt and lack of confidence. Rituals enable you to take all of the previously harnessed powerful & positive behaviors and thoughts with you as you move forward on your life path.

When you see someone like Beyonce, Tony Robbins or T.D. Jakes, you are looking at someone who has engaged in a serious daily ritual. Whether that ritual is consistent exercise, a powerful prayer life or intentional practice of your craft, the ritual allows them to consistently produce successful results.

Rituals help us not only develop muscle memory, but mindset memory that enables us to replicate positive results at will. While my mother's routine of cleaning the house was great for Sundays, because there was no ritual (intention) behind it, it could not be replicated at will. Hence, our disdain for chores every other day of the week.

By turning our routines into rituals, us Mamas become the masters of our own fate. We know that all we need to do is to turn on the ritual to ignite the behaviors, feelings and thoughts necessary to accomplish our goal.

We see it all the time on television. The writer needs to pin down and finish his book so he goes to a cabin in the woods. That's a ritual. The athlete is getting ready for a big game, so he trains vigorously for weeks. That's a ritual. The dad wants to bond with his son so they go camping. That's a ritual.

Rituals not only give intention to our daily lives, but they provide signals for behaviors. The importance of physical orientation in ritual is that it gets us ready to produce the real thing.

I light incense to help me when I'm writing, reading or just thinking. No matter where I am. If I smell incense, I automatically go into philosophical mode. As we talked about before, burning incense is a ritual that started long before I was born in the temples that dotted African origination from South Africa to Egypt. This ritual withstands the test of time.

Rituals are powerful, without them, you are powerless.

Rituals All Around You

I find it ironic how so many Brown Mamas unknowingly engage in routines that really are rituals. Rituals are simply routines with intention behind them.

The Brown Mama Mindset

Because our African ancestors arrived on these shores carrying a culture that had been in existence for no less than 10,000 years prior to encountering any European or Asiatic people, we arrived with our own rituals as well.

Of course, during the hells of slavery we were forced to suppress our own rituals, and made to adopt those of our oppressors. But, we've always been an intelligent and crafty people. Our ancestors found ways to secretly pass on the rituals learned in the Motherland.

For that reason, many of us Brown Mamas unknowingly engage in rituals every day.

African activist and philosopher, Marimba Ani, details many of the rituals that African women participate in unknowingly in her book, Let the Circle be Unbroken.

A few of the modern rituals that African people engage in include ripping on each other, or playing the dozens.

According to Ani, it turns out all those "Yo Mama" jokes are actually derived from a Zulu marriage ritual that still exist in modern South Africa. In-laws from both sides of a Zulu family will exchange insults in order to clear the air before the marriage ceremony. It was believed that allowing each side of the family to express their dislike for the other before the marriage commitment was sealed led to stronger family relations and ties after the marriage as each side had a chance to say their peace.

Another ritual unknowingly being performed by Brown Mamas includes the stretching of the baby's limbs. I remember when I brought my first son home from the hospital. My mother made sure I stretched out his arms and legs daily as a way to get him ready to walk. This tradition is actually derived from an African Yoruba ritual called Nna. Ani describes it as "a learning experience in which the mother exposes the baby to new sensations so that she might begin to be aware of herself as a distinct and yet dependent entity."

In addition, many Brown Mamas burn incense in their homes not realizing the ritual of bundling and burning incense in the early African temples of Punt. Punt was located in modern day Somalia. The temples of Somalia, Sudan and Egypt burned incense all day as a way of welcoming in the God of their ancestors. The Catholic Church replicated this ritual when they encountered our ancestors and now use it in their churches to worship and usher in their god.

Yet, many of us Brown Mamas burn incense not knowing that our ancestors and Creator are waiting at the door to be welcomed in as we engage in a ritual that served as doormat for their presence for thousands of years.

Then there's the colors that spring up every Sunday morning in the front pew of the church. In traditionally, Baptist Black churches every Sunday morning women walk into the Lord's house wearing shades of yellow, pops of purple, hats with feathers, flowers, lace and everything in between. Our African ancestors did the same during ceremonies that were designed to usher in the spirits of our ancestors to help correct or celebrate happenings in the village. The vibrancy of color, uniqueness of style and excitement to be present, dressed and 'in your right mind,' was also expressed.

As Mamas operating with a Brown Mama Mindset we must become women who take our daily behaviors much more seriously. We must become Mamas who see the importance of remembering who we are, expressing our own cultural uniqueness in the world, and passing down our rituals to our children so that our culture, belief systems and individuality is not forgotten.

The problem with routines that are never made into rituals is that they are taken for granted. How many times have you engaged in Nna, or "the stretching," with your babies and not realized the power of that ritual. You possessed the spiritual, collective power of your ancestors in that moment, but were not able to harness the power because you were unaware of it.

Not acknowledging the power that you have as an African mother is like inheriting a million dollars and then locking your inheritance in a closet never to be utilized. During Nna you could have been speaking words over your child about their uniqueness, encouraging them on their life path and reminding him/her of the power that exist within.

The Creator is waiting for us Brown Mamas to tap into the rituals and collective wisdom of our ancestors. The kitchen prowess that your grandmother possessed is waiting for you in ritual. The entrepreneurial mindset of your great uncle is waiting for you in ritual. The love, intellect, fierceness and boldness of spirit and every other characteristic you yearn to integrate into your life and persona are waiting for you in ritual.

How do I create ritual?

The answer: however you'd like. It's really that simple. Remember, a ritual is simply a routine with intention and faith behind it. That's all.

One of my most treasured rituals is taking a walk around my neighborhood in the morning. I walk around my block 3 times. I clear my mind by singing a song or remembering the spirit of my grandfathers and grandmothers, or sometimes I just listen to my own thoughts. Then I come back in the house, light an incense and say a prayer to the Creator that I continue to have a positive mindset.

With my children we do a ritual of daily affirmation. We affirm ourselves as African people, as kind and respected leaders in our community and as trailblazers of a new reality for African people.

My husband and I have a monthly ritual of reviewing our life's purpose on the first day of each month.

Rituals should be meaningful, easy to do, and most of all, intentional. That's it.

There's nothing spooky. You don't have to be an old African woman who sits around surrounded by melting candles, herbs and room with beads on the entrance. You are an individual. Your life rituals should be just as unique as you are.

What is important is that your rituals are intentional, and that you can pass them down to your children and grandchildren with ease.

So, don't stress over it. Just like my mother's Sunday cleaning routine, you may already have a routine in place that can easily be turned into a ritual with a little more intention and good heaping of faith.

Mama Map Invitation

Develop a ritual. Use your *Mama Map Workbook* to document your routines and come up with a ritual that can become a tradition in your family.

Section III: LOVE

Chapter 11

Blame Game

"Stop walking around here like your sh*t don't stink."
-Said by every Black mom everywhere

Black women are always complaining about Black men. I remember being a teenager and hearing all of the women in my family complain, at some point or another, about all the problems men had caused in their lives. And often, I was among the women complaining. From a baby's dad who didn't pay child support to niggas staying out late all night. Although the complaints were mostly valid, I just remember thinking "Why do we even bother with them."

The Brown Mama Mindset

If you've ever joined the Black woman, Black man dating pool, you'll understand that there are many reasons Black women should just leave Black men alone altogether. Many Black men have problems remaining employed, don't have blueprints for fatherhood, can barely pay their own bills let alone pay yours too, and a good number of them have some serious issues with monogamy. Who could blame a sistah for dating men from other ethnic backgrounds, or staying single? From some of our sistah's points-of-view, any man is better than the constant insecurity of sustaining a relationship, or worse, trying to find a relationship with a Black man.

Nevertheless, 10 years ago I married a Black man. I never thought I'd get married because of the tumultuous, soap-opera style relationships I had with men in my past. Everything we talked about in that former paragraph, well it all happened to me too. I was cheated on by my son's father before our baby even exited my womb, I engaged in a series of relationships with men who can't even pronounce monogamy, and so on.

Blame Game

The Wall

Needless to say, when I married my husband I'd securely built a 10-foot wall to ensure that if anyone survived the relationship without hurt feelings, it was going to be me.

My husband and I were very different.

I was mean. My husband was kind.

We married when I was already 8 months with child. Regardless, I wore a halter-top style white as snow wedding dress, with a train that was about 1-foot long. He said I looked beautiful, but I couldn't accept the compliment, I did not believe him.

He cried on our wedding day. He said that he'd known he was going to marry me from the moment we met. I did not have those feelings, or even the capacity to understand those feelings at that time, but I said "I do," and moved to his hometown of Brooklyn, New York with him one month later. I was terrified.

I'd never been taught how to be a wife. I had only glamorized the wedding day in my mind like so many girls do. I gave very little thought to what life would look like in the days, weeks, months, years, and decades ahead. Once I was officially married, I was like, "wait the hell up", somebody tricked me. Marriage was not at all like what I'd seen glamorized on TV.

I arrived in New York City no more of a wife or even a woman then I'd been the day I turned 18.

I could only cook in mimic style, copying the recipes I'd seen the women in my family make during big family dinners. My husband was Trinidadian. The southern-style, fatty foods I knew how to cook were no good for him. I've always been good at cleaning the house because my preference is toward neatness, but what I was utterly unprepared for -was giving a home warmth. I had no idea how to make a man feel warm when he came home from work and my husband worked so, so hard.

And intimacy. I had no idea what real intimacy was. It was sex for me. My previous relationships had caused me to completely remove any feelings from sex. We could have sex and argue 10 minutes later.

My own immaturity caused me to deflect in arguments. Nothing was ever my fault. The 10-foot wall I built insured that every argument was a referendum on his faults and he felt it. In the two

Blame Game

years after we married, my husband gained 50 lbs., sprouted grey hairs in the front of his head and was just plain ole exhausted.

He was holding on to me by thin strands of thread. I was the woman he loved unconditionally. He never argued with me. Never threw my food in the garbage and made love to me as if every time was the first time. But, the wall.

You know the wall very well. Black women know the wall. It's the wall we build after sexual abuse and too many broken hearts. We build the wall because daddy never came back home, mama had to go to work and the community around us was nothing but concrete and empty beer bottles.

We build the wall with ambition. You know, the sistahs who have 5 degrees, but can't cook. We build the wall with serial dating. The sistahs who refuse to take time to heal and do inner-work before jumping into her third relationship this year. We even build the wall with our children. Our mamas who spend so much time raising their kids that they never form any hobbies, have no idea what they even want in a man and barely have any sistah friends to enjoy life with. Us Brown Mamas, we know the wall very, very well.

The Brown Mama Mindset

Sometimes I wonder how different the early years of my marriage would have been had I not put up that wall as a girl. I wonder if those conversations about Black men that I heard as a child would be relevant if the women having them had even acknowledged that the wall they'd put up was equally responsible for their relationship woes.

I love my sistahs, but there are just some things we need to come clean about.

We have to begin to tear down this wall because we KNOW that a person is not capable of seeing the beauty inside of us unless we see it in ourselves first. We cannot possibly see the *potential* inside of ourselves behind the wall we've built up.

Both Black men and Black women have a wall up. Black men AND women are broken. We hate each other because we both live in the same cage. Rather than realizing that we are in this together we turn on each other. We talk bad about each other. We fight. We air our dirty laundry on the nightly news, hood corners and Facebook in-living-color production at the feet of other races and ethnicities and get mad when they call us n*ggas. Well honey, you get what you pay for.

Blame Game

Here's the Truth Mama...

It is time for Black women to decide to take a long look in the mirror, admit our faults and forgive ourselves.

Yes, we are owed an apology from Black men. Yes, we have borne the burden and effects of our slave masters actions upon our race. There is no doubt about it. Period.

But so many of us have internalized the behaviors our former slave masters forced on us, that we don't even know we are living a lie. We tell ourselves that we beat our kids because if we don't do it the world will. Is it right for us to cause *our* Brown Babies mental and physical damage first so that the world won't do it? Huh? Really? That makes no sense.

We tell ourselves that our men are incapable. Rather than allowing them to be men, we often fight with them and don't trust their decision-making capabilities. We actively work against them all while tearing down our own homes, just so we can be in charge. But, guess what sis? **You still ain't in charge. You're just in control.** And, you're running yourself ragged trying to keep all the balls in a straight line.

The Brown Mama Mindset

If your baby's dad is irresponsible, let him be who he is. Stop arguing with him about things you know he won't do. Be accountable for your own actions. Acting in your female essence means understanding you can only control your own actions, thoughts and emotions. By trying to live for everyone else all you do is stress yourself out.

We tell ourselves the lie that everything in a relationship should be 50/50. No, a successful relationship (in marriage, or otherwise) is each person giving 100% and staying in their lane. You were not made a woman simply because you have longer hair, a vagina and less physical strength. Stop allowing the narrow-minded definitions of the role of a woman that are common in Western society, determine how you value your beautifully feminine mind and mystique.

A huge part of our dysfunction is that we don't know how to operate in feminine power.

There is a certain type of power associated with being a woman. Mamas operating in a Brown Mama Mindset know our power doesn't come from how many jobs we can hold down, degrees we can obtain, sexual partners we can have or how many arguments we can win.

A woman with a Brown Mama Mindset understands her power comes from grace, style, warmth, the diligence of her hands, and her capacity to soften the blow of her intellectual strength so that thoughts of her great mind linger in a room long after her physical has taken flight.

Us ladies with a Brown Mama Mindset use our intuition as a guide in daily life and take time EVERYDAY to do what is essential for our own sanity. A woman is both the substance of the cake itself and the frilly, frailty of its icing. Women keep the tempo of life. We are behind the scenes not because we are not worthy of being seen, but because we are the life-giving essence of our homes and communities. Without us, family life ceases to exist, therefore we reserve the right and opt for the security and protection we deserve.

That is what our slave masters took away from us. They took away our security and forced us to be on the frontlines for our men. We really think it's normal for a woman to be loud, boisterous and flamboyant.

No honey, the woman is the ultimate hunter and predator. Like female lions, we are not to be seen until we are ready to pounce on our prey. Women work in the shadows as the spirit protectors, guidance and mysteriously, devious and brilliant female minds of their households and communities.

It is only once the gazelle is gasping for air that it thinks "Damn I let that bitch get me." Brown Mamas need to engage in this same way. It is not important that we are seen, it is important that we are felt.

Broken Black Man = Broken Black Woman

One question we need to illuminate is: If our men are doing so bad, just how good could we possibly be doing?

If our men are cheaters, what does that say about our ability and capacity to give and accept love? If our daddies are rolling stones, do we really even know what a good man looks like having only experienced the lack of or distorted versions of our own daddies? It's time for us to reevaluate if we even have the necessary knowledge to decide what a good man is.

Blame Game

If our communities are composed of nothing but liquor stores, churches and food desert-like corner stores do we really know what being 'rich' even means? Do we have a correct estimation of the concept of wealth and its longevity? Wealth is a state of mind. It is a way of being raised with a standard of living that is beneficial to not just you as an individual, but to a group of people that you call family, community and society. Wealth is inherited, not earned. You can only have wealth if you have first birthed a spirit and mind of wealth within your state of being.

I say it again; Black men *and* women are sick.

We are the ultimate ying and yang. Together, we are mighty and a force not to be tempted. God didn't make man and women so dependent upon each other for no reason.

But, without one another, we are exposed and weakened. Apart we *are* able to function, but easily swayed toward dysfunction. That is the dilemma of Black men and women operating outside of their full gender realization and strengths.

As fully realized men and women we understand the necessity of dependency between male and female that exist as a rule of law here on Earth. However, outside of that understanding we manifest warped roles of what it means to be man and woman.

Black women and men are in the middle of a great gender neglect crisis. Neither of us has a good idea of how to proceed in a way that will inform or give instruction to our children on how to best raise up more Black children. We've never asked ourselves the question: What happens to our feminine and masculine energies when they are not allowed to be adequately expressed?

What happens when boys can't learn to hunt? What happens when girls never learn to sew? What happens in a young woman's womb when she is constantly told by the elders in her community not to have children? Spoken vibrations have physical consequences. What happens in the psyche, and scrotum, of a young, Black man when he is constantly told that the women who look like him are not worthy of his seed and should be disrespected? What happens when a woman is so hardened that she can walk past children in her own community who are hungry and hurting and feel nothing? What happens when a man can collect tithes at his church then walk into a barren, hopeless community, hop in his Bentley and drive to his neighborhood 10 miles away without blinking an eye? And most importantly, how does viewing all of this affect the minds of our now wealth-seeking children? How do they now view wealth? How do they now view you?

The gender neglect that is plaguing Black men and women is apparent in our inability to forge successful male-female alliances that can be continuously replicated by our children.

Despite our current despair, we need only look to our African ancestors for clues on how to regain the complementarity that was once expressed so marvelously between Black men and women.

In Ancient Sierra Leone culture, women had very specific ways in which they expressed their female energy. Many cultures hold traditions that instruct women in how they are to dress in order to show their goddess prowess as a part of their community.

The secret Sande Society, which still exist today, of Sierra Leone instructs their young girls in rituals that equate to a successful and respected womanhood later in life. The teachings include everything from intimacy rituals, to rites of passage for women and instructions on crossing over into the realm of becoming a revered female elder.

Sande women even engage in specific activities that directly identify not only their unique feminine power within their village, but also their status in the village. African women built institutions within their tribes that addressed the issues, ideas and daily lives of single women, married women, elder women and puberty aged women. In essence, being a woman once meant something.

These Sande traditions (as well as the Mende traditions for men) prepared the ladies of Sierra Leone to go into their relationships with full confidence in their ability to be good wives and productive members of this community. Even to this day, there are many political position in Sierra Leone that can only be filled by Sande women and Mende men.

But, what happens when a woman is abruptly or even gradually is stripped of these guides? Where then does she express or form outlet for feminine energy that was once allowed to flow freely. I can't answer this question fully, I can only tell you of my own experiences.

Blame Game

When I was unable to garden to gain the connection I now experience in my Godspace, I was dependent upon the pastor at church for a second-hand God experience. Without the positive intimacy of being in a healthy relationship, I ran to night clubs. Devoid of a communal space where I could express and gain physical substance from my God-given talents, I got degrees, worked dead-end, uninspiring jobs and lived each day on the go as a horse on the cowboy's Western prairie.

Without rituals, feminine institutions and standards that would assist me in making the ultimate, uninterrupted, one-on-one connection to the Most High and the whole of creation, all of my actions led to more non-living actions.

Rather than continuing this cycle of Black women blaming Black men for their problems and Black men blaming Black women for their problems, we need to realize the gender neglect and broken social systems that have led to the dysfunction in our relationships.

Dead emotions, behaviors and mentalities just beget more dead emotions, behaviors and mentalities. If we are going to move beyond the lackluster relationships with our children's fathers and mates that we are used to, we are going to have to start to engage in living thoughts and living actions.

We are going to have to begin to breathe life into our men, and they into us. Even when it's hard, we must be patient with our children's fathers and husbands realizing that he may be engaging in dead actions that are not capable of producing living results. The answer is not to continue to go lower with him, but to rise above his low tempo by producing within ourselves the living actions that will, hopefully, resuscitate his comatose state in time.

Jesus said it best when he said in Mark 5:13, "You are the salt of the earth. But if the salt loses its saltiness, how can it be made salty again?" You must be the salt in all your relationships. In this way you are continuing on the path of the person you are destined to be, and as you walk you are giving life to the dead who follow you.

Be accountable for yourself. Begin to examine and make right the paths in your own heart and mind.

It was not until I accepted this as truth that my relationship with my son's father begin to turn in a positive direction. Prior to developing my Brown

Blame Game

Mama Mindset of self-authenticity and accountability, my son's father and I would have shouting matches over the phone and couldn't stand to be in one another's presence.

Once I accepted that there was nothing I could do to help him to change his ways besides be unabashedly truthful with myself about my actions, thoughts and interactions with him, we bloomed a friendship. We bloomed a friendship based on love for our child, accountability for our actions and mutual respect for the lives of each other.

So, let's get back in line mamas.

If your relationship is tinged with tension, start showing the same kindness and patience you exhibit with your children, friends or co-workers with your husband. In the words of my mother, "Kill 'em with kindness."

If you are lonely in spirit and have not found a place to fully express your feminine energy, it's time to get authentic with yourself. Go back to Chapter 1, get off the treadmill and begin a deep inner-quest to find out where your talents lie and what truly makes you happy.

If you can't cook, then it's up to you to get a cookbook. If your house is unkempt, then it's time to do some tidying. The home is a reflection of the female mental state.

And, for God's sake, if the lovin' ain't right, you better get some lingerie, turn on some soft music, have a bottle of wine and bring that ole' thing back.

Accountability allows us to love from the inside out. Blame makes us unaware of ourselves, and stops us from seeing the goodness in others.

If you've never accepted responsibility for an argument in your relationship you are not accountable for yourself. If every disagreement turns into a battle of you vs. him, rather than how can we make this right so we can move on, then you both have some serious heart work to do.

Years ago, I began a battle to get to know myself. Some days have been hard, others have been easy. But, it feels so good to love my husband for who he is. My love for him is no longer based on how he makes me feel. My love for him is simply a reflection of how much I care for myself. I love him out of the joy reservoir that I've created for my inner being.

Blame Game

I've done this by being accountable for my actions and learning to forgive myself for building the wall and neglecting my feminine spirit. Rather than looking to him to fill the void that I created, I am an active pursuant of my own needs and wants. I realize that every action and thought I have was formulated in my own heart. Therefore, there is never anyone else responsible for me.

Now, my relationship is not a competition it is a complementarity. Sometimes I do what my husband tells me to do, and sometimes he does what I tell him to do. We approach each disagreement from the standpoint of doing what's best for ourselves and for our relationship.

I've adopted the Brown Mama Mindset of doing the inner work of taking down the wall. Brown Mamas would do well to find out why we built the wall in the first place, and brick by brick release ourselves from the inner turmoil that causes sour relationships and mean hearts like the one I used to have.

At some point Black women have to accept that we have a role to play in those relationships gone bad. Whether we've served as the doormat or the instigator, we have to accept that just as Black women have had broken hearts, minds, souls and spirits, Black men do too.

Mama Map Invitation

Let's get really authentic about who we are and who we want to be in the **right** relationship. Use your *Mama Map Workbook* to create the perfect you.

Chapter 12

Insecure

"All my life men have told me I wasn't pretty enough. Even the men I was dating... It's always been men putting me down, even my dad. To this day, when someone says I'm cute, I can't see it. I don't see it no matter what anybody says." -Lil' Kim

It takes time for a woman to become comfortable with being her real self all the time. I remember meeting my childhood best friend for the first time. She was this chocolate, 5'2", chunky chick who had all the confidence in the world. All the cute boys in our class were her friends. She exuded a kind of "Imma be me" attitude that I always wished I'd had.

At 13-years-old I was always second guessing myself, as most teenage girls are. Although, I'm now sure my bestie was doing the same, at the time it just didn't seem like it. Through the European-centric lens of America, my bestie's brown skin and curvaceous figure were not 'ideal.' But, you couldn't tell her that! Belly-shirts, short skirts and fitted dresses were regulars in her closet and she always looked cute in them. That type of self-assurance made me so proud to have her as my best friend.

She was the exact opposite of me.

For all of my teenage years, twenties and the first few years of my thirties I was what I like to call systemically insecure. It didn't matter that through that same Euro-centric lens my light skin, small frame and narrow nose made my beauty 'ideal'. I didn't see it.

From the time I was 13 until I was 32, I'd only had one friend, and not because no one wanted to be my friend either. I was just guarded.

Most times, I'd choose loneliness over friendships. I didn't want to be lonely. I just wasn't comfortable being exposed. My deep insecurity manifested itself in my fear of letting people get to know the real me.

Insecure

So much of building friendships as a woman is about full exposure. Most of us Mamas have a real need for genuine friendships, but our insecurity keeps us from developing those type of relationships.

One reason I started a support group for Black moms, Brown Mamas, was due to my need to make friends.

Just like me, most Brown Mamas are yearning for friendship. Not surface friendship, but deep, meaningful, trusting relationships that go beyond girl's night out and expands into 'tell me ya business and I'll tell you mines' territory. The biggest barrier to real friendship is lack of trust.

Most Mamas will agree that it's hard to find a friend we can trust, right? But, as I get older I find that the exact opposite is actually true. Most people will let you know what you can and can't trust them with in the initial stages of building a relationship through their actions. Like Oprah said, "When someone tells you who they are, listen".

But, here's the revelation I've had over the last few years: Building solid, deep friendships is not just about finding a friend you can trust. It's all about being able to **trust yourself enough to be the true you** within the friendship.

This is where deep insecurity enters the picture.

Some Brown Mamas cannot engage in real friendships because we fear exposing our low self-esteem. From that space of low self-worth, we cannot be happy for another Mama and are not comfortable being the truest version of ourselves at all times. In other words, we don't feel safe with ourselves, and therefore do not feel safe in our relationships. This is called insecurity.

Insecurity is the constant internal demeaning of your own authentic thoughts, feelings and behaviors. The daughters of insecurity are pessimism, negative thoughts & emotions, unforgiveness of self & others, discouragement and the constant thought & feeling that you deserve less.

Insecurity is a pattern of thinking that traps us Brown Mamas into loneliness, anxiety and fear. We lack nothing, but we believe we lack everything.

This is why insecurity can wreak so much havoc on a person's life, because when your intuition, or "inner-tuition", becomes your "inner-bill" it will literally suck you dry.

Insecure

Just like a bill due at the end of the month, insecurity takes the deposit of every positive thought (paycheck), hope, dream and even accomplishment that you have in your mind (or bank) and snatches it right out at the end of the month. The raping of your inner paycheck leaves you with a positive thought deficit as you enter each day and new cycle of your life.

Through insecurity your intuition can turn into an internal mechanism that preys on everything positive you wish to be in your life. Insecurity roots out and kills positive thoughts that push you towards your purpose.

Developing a Brown Mama Mindset is the exact opposite. It means making it your first priority to rid yourself of insecurity every single day.

You will do this by evaluating your negative thoughts so that you might begin to abolish them.

Brown Mamas must realize that we are 360 degrees of a whole person. You are 180 degrees of a persona that is agreeable with humanity and in harmony, but you are also 180 degrees of a disagreeable personality that tends to be less harmonious seeking fruits of a lesser spirit like materialism, manipulation and greed. Despite the equality of these dualities, you are capable of tipping the scale. Positive thoughts that manifest into fruit-bearing actions are how you give favor to your more agreeable persona.

When you become a purveyor of your thoughts and begin to speak life in places where negativity once ruled, you tip the balance in favor or your agreeable self. The agreeable side of you then begins to attract and complement the agreeable spirit inside of the people you meet, and circumstances you encounter. Just as you can attract joy, peace and love, you can attract a secure mindset and lifestyle.

I would venture to say that everything you've ever wanted to be in your life is sitting on the other side of ridding yourself of insecurity.

Possessing a Brown Mama Mindset means trusting yourself enough to know what is right for you. Once you've tipped the balance toward your more agreeable self your 'inner tuition' is literally pushing you toward accomplishing your goals, being a good parent, loving your mate and nourishing your inner-self. AND, it is simultaneously drawing more goodness your way.

Having a Brown Mama Mindset is about being okay with being honest with yourself about what makes you feel good and what makes you feel not-so-good, and being willing to love yourself through it all.

Unprotected

Being a Brown Mama in America is like wearing a guaranteed badge of the unprotected. I've heard Mamas say many a day that they feel like bad experiences and people are just drawn to them.

I used to agree with them until I realized that you always find predators where the prey is present. While we Mamas are certainly responsible for maintaining our own positive mindsets, there is something to be said for the systematic lack of protection that Black women are born into.

So many Mamas are born into fatherless homes and man-less communities that it's no surprise that we are more likely to be sexually exploited, give birth to children before we are mentally prepared, get STDs, and end up living a life of poverty.

Sometimes we forget that when psychological trauma is allowed to go unchecked generation after generation, it affects us on a cellular level and leads to mental damage that can be passed down to our children. Joy Degruy speaks about this in her book *Post-Traumatic Slave Disorder*.

In her book, Degruy makes the case that Black women, and men, are suffering from mental illness due to the generations of torture that was inflicted upon African people. She says: "You can't have 246 years of trauma, and expect there not to be more trauma. Especially, if those 246 years of trauma was followed by more trauma."

Degruy is absolutely right. For generations upon generations Black women were raped, scared straight as child after child after child was sold and ripped from her arms, experimented on by doctors and just mentally traumatized by the horrors of slavery, and as Degruy says we were never given therapy.

Therefore, insecurity has damn near become the birthright of the Brown Mama.

From birth most of us are taught not to expect too much out of life. We are taught that life is going to be hard, and that it's our job to just deal with it.

But the truth is Mama, we are the liberators we seek because we possess the hearts and minds of the First Queens.

Something I have not shared with you is that before my 5-year journey toward raising my self-esteem and conquering my mind to develop a Brown Mama Mindset, I began studying my African roots intensely.

I studied books like *Radiance from the Sun* by Sandra Boone, *African People in World History* by John Henrike Clark, and *The Afrikan Origins of Civilization* by Chiekh Anta Diop. I wanted to erase the thought in my mind that the only history I had to look back upon was that of torture and despair, or as some call it the Maafa.

After learning about the many queens, sages and female goddesses of my African ancestors a spring of confidence began to well up in me. I realized that just like my African ancestors, there were no boundaries that I could not break.

Just as Queen Hatshepsut, Tiye and Nzinga, I was capable of bringing entire nations, white and Black, to their knees with my wit, female prowess and grace.

I read and listened to the many, many, many stories of my ancestors and rediscovered my security.

I searched my family tree so that I could begin to draw upon the wisdom and good character of the grandmothers, grandfathers and great grandmothers that came before me.

By taking the time to mourn for the African slaves who endured so that I could live today and celebrate the great ancestry that came before them, I formed a better understanding of the generational curses that were playing themselves out in my life. I also, gained a new narrative that I could draw wisdom and joy from as I create a new reality for myself and my family.

Now, my security comes from the same essence that was planted in the first quote you read in this book - "Time was."

I regained my inner-security with the realization that I am limitless. Not time, not space, not even this Earth can fully contain all of the power my soul holds when I'm to connect to my ancestral greatness.

I am constantly surrounded by the protective energies of the Creator and those who come before me. The energy that I possess in my soul was intentionally passed to me. It cannot be duplicated and will never die, or lose its power.

As Oprah says, I realize that when I walk into a room I carry all of my ancestors with me. Through this empowering fact, I am constantly able to Sankofa – go back and fetch the greatness of my past to utilize in the hope and security of my future.

I encourage all Brown Mamas to take that backward stroll toward their ancestral avatar. Take some time to glean the knowledge, wisdom and joy from the ancestors who came before you.

For Mothers of Sons

It's easy to fall prey to promiscuity when you are insecure and unprotected. That year, at 23 years-old was the loneliest year I've ever had. Being promiscuous was the only thing I thought would cure the numbness I felt.

That year, there was nothing about me that I felt good about. I had gained about 15 pounds, I had no hair and wore a lot of wigs and weaves to compensate, and just felt like I had nothing to offer the world.

By that time, I'd stopped going to nightclubs with friends and started going alone because I was there so frequently. On the night I couldn't go clubbing to numb the pain of my insecurity, I'd smoke weed and listen to Amy Winehouse until my eyes were so red and swollen from crying that I couldn't do anything except go to sleep.

In the summer prior to that year I had an abortion and felt so barren inside. The moment that baby was ripped from my womb I felt nothing, but nothing. On top of that, my stepfather, who was my father through my entire childhood, died brutally. Besides my mother, who was struck with grief herself, I had no one to talk to about it. My stepdad's family treated my sisters and I as if we didn't matter. It gave me a feeling of resentment and anger that I'm not quite sure I've dealt with even to this day.

Being young and ill-equipped in managing my negative thoughts, I was depressed and discouraged. It showed on the inside and the outside of me. Love didn't live with me anymore.

That year I cried myself to sleep just about every night, my home looked like a disaster zone and my mind was a fertile ground for negativity.

Insecure

I was insecure and unprotected.

Up until I met my husband, no man had ever shown me how to be properly loved. No man had ever protected me, or stood up for me, or even just stood for me. I was a fatherless daughter turned unprotected Black woman.

Now, as a mother of 3 boys I am determined to change this narrative. We Mamas can change this narrative by teaching our boys how they should be interacting with the girls and women in their lives.

In the famous song *Flawless* by Beyonce, the extraordinary poet Chimamanda Ngozi Adichie asked the question: Why do we teach girls to aspire to marriage, but we don't teach boys the same?

This question sums up, in its very essence, the reason Black women are relegated to a status of the most unprotected women in America. It's simple: We (both mothers and fathers) have not raised up men to protect ourselves or our other womenfolk.

This leads to the systemic insecurity that we possess. Yes, our insecurity is certainly a product of discouragement and negative thoughts, but it has also been built upon the back of our status as unprotected.

We feel insecure because we have either formerly, or currently, had no security. We come from fatherless and husbandless homes. We live in communities where police and criminals alike are allowed to roam with immunity killing and sexually exploiting our daughters.

The question us Brown Mamas need to begin to ask ourselves is, "How much better would my life had been if I would've had a competent, loving father to raise, rear and guide me in life?"

If you answered, "A hell of a lot better," then you are at the starting point of understanding what characteristics to encourage in your sons in order to prevent the next generation of girls from growing up fatherless. Here are a few characteristics I try to encourage in my sons.

Chivalry

Opening doors is dead. Make sure our sons enter rooms before their women to make sure it is safe before she enters. Teach our sons how to protect the women and girls in their lives. Make them aware of safety procedures in their homes and in places they frequent. Always remind them that rule of thumb in Black communities is that women and children are always first.

Chastity

Let's teach our sons that value is more important than variety when courting women. We have a rule with our teenage boy; he is only allowed to be interested in one girl at a time. We believe this teaches him to choose wisely and to be sure to value the time, personality and soul of every girl he encounters.

Investment

Teaching our sons that a relationship is an investment, you get out of it what you put in. If you are kind, careful and genuine with a woman she will return that love. Also teach our sons that Black women are worth the investment. Let them know that our social systems in Black communities are broken and in need of repair, but that if he is willing to love unconditionally the right woman will love him back.

Boundaries

Teaching our sons that women are allowed to say no, and they should only have to say no once for you to understand. Also, teach our sons that women should not be expected to respond immediately to their advances. Show our sons that girls are allowed and should 'play hard to get', or simply create standards and rules for the boys they choose to date.

As Mamas of brown boys who are so capable of being the strong and secure protectors of our communities that we need, it is our responsibility to help our young men understand their role as the gatekeepers of the women in their communities.

It is also important that we begin to possess a Brown Mama Mindset that acknowledges our sons as the protectors of our communities. While we may be dealing with an issue of fatherlessness ourselves, we can certainly think of the characteristics our fathers lacked and begin talking to our sons. More importantly, we must teach out sons the very behaviors we hope they will inherit in order to protect the women and girls in their lives.

As we'll talk about in Chapter 14: Parenting the Black Way, we must begin to parent our children in a way that helps them to be the problem solvers of the issues they will inherit tomorrow.

Brown Mamas are in the unique position of being the knowledge holders and teachers that can determine a change in protection-status for the Black girls of the next generation.

Mama Map Invitation

Let's do an insecurity assessment. Using your *Mama Map Workbook* let's access and log our daily thoughts to be authentic about our current state of security, or lack thereof.

Chapter 13

To Be Loved

"No journey is too great when one finds what he seeks."
-Prince Akeem in Coming to America

Y'all already know that I was a mean wife, but what ya'll don't know is the depth of the love my husband has for me. How my husband and I survived our first two years of marriage was a mystery to me for a period of time.

At 26 years-old the love my husband had for me was tangible, it was real, and it hit a chord in my soul that had never been struck. My husband's unconditional love changed the condition of my heart, mind and soul. His steadfastness, long-suffering, harmony seeking love forced a change in me; a difficult change, but a lovely change nonetheless.

True love is like a mirror for the soul. When someone loves you despite your craziness, mood swings and unrighteous justifications, over time this kind of love has a way of making you look internally. Every time I'd start a fight my husband would only work to diffuse the argument.

When I would overspend, he never reprimanded me, or cut off my access to money, he'd just keep going to work. He kept loving and being kind to me. Every time I'd make some stupid mistake that the entire family had to pay for, he'd just help me make it right.

At the end of every crooked road, there I stood with only the breadcrumbs of my own faults to look at. Like they say, everywhere you go, there you are. Because my husband had never played the game with me and had never reciprocated my madness, there was no one else to blame. His kindness had become a reflection for me to view my own insecurity and bad habits.

To Be Loved

With my husband's love I stopped seeking to be right and began seeking to listen more. His genuine care for my well being made me more patient with my children and willing to understand their perspectives. My man's love helped the 'me' that had been buried since childhood shine again. His love did not complete me, but his love did free me.

It freed me from the thought that I deserved the consequence of not being loved. It opened me up to receive love, and once my love cup began to overflow, I became one who could freely give love.

This is the kind of love that us Brown Mamas deserve. We deserve to be loved in a way that opens us up. We deserve to be loved in a way that releases us from the thought of relationship conditions and consequences. We deserve to be loved through our madness and mistakes. We deserve to bloom into women who can give love from the overflow of that which has been given to us.

So many of us are currently operating on a love wavelength that incorrectly defines what the experience of love should look and feel like. We've misinterpreted control, carelessness, lust, materialism and inconsistency for love. In actuality, love is genuine care and concern for another's natural state of well-being. It is friendship, consistency, freedom of self-expression, healing and patience.

When we incorrectly define love, we spend an enormous amount of time trying to be the girl that is wanted. We dress the part, attempt to act the part, temper our personalities and points-of-view, and even design our friendships around creating the ideal circumstances for finding a man.

When a Mama is properly loved this is no longer required. When we are loved properly a sense of freedom is gained. The need to be wanted disappears and all that is left is the need *to be*.

True love frees up space in a woman for self-expression, confident vulnerability, self-reflection and an inner-confidence that has life-transforming powers.

Brown Mamas need to become aware of the spiritual and physical awakening that could occur in us when we are loved the right way.

An unloved woman is like a seed buried in the dirt. She has all the potential of being a full bloomed flower, but no one has nurtured or cared for her. She lacks the rain, sunlight and air necessary to grow.

However, when a woman is loved properly by a man the seed within her activates. Masculine love compliments our female personality and allows a new side, a different version of our minds, emotions and even our physical bodies to activate.

I loved to write before I met my husband, but without his constant encouragement and belief in me, I would not have written this book. When I mastered my job, and knew my soul was yearning to manifest something greater, it was my husband who stayed up late with me writing grant applications and refining my business plan. His consistent backup and re-assurance has given me the confidence of a million Kanye Wests.

I lacked nothing when I met my husband, but his love made me supremely aware and confident in my strengths. Equally important, his love allowed me the freedom of knowing I didn't need to do everything for everybody. He was there to close the gap in the areas I was not able to perform in.

When a Mama knows without a shadow of a doubt that regardless of whether she succeeds or fails, her man will be there to back her up, she's willing to jump off any ledge into the arms of him who loves her.

Love should be a secure safety net that crosses out fears, and provides a stable landing for hopes moved to action.

Find Peace. Love Will Find You

Just as optimism is the daughter of joy, peace is the daughter of love. Mama, I wish I could awaken you to the power of vibration.

Every thought has weight, shape, color and form, size, quality and power. The thoughts that you emit at every moment of each day are either propelling your desires further from you, or pulling them closer to you.

Focusing your energy on your lack of ability to find a loving, romantic relationship is not helping you find love. On the contrary, developing a Brown Mama Mindset that allows you the time, space and experiences necessary to cultivate self-love and a true understanding of what genuine love should look like are agreeable behaviors that draw "the one" closer to you.

Love is a desire that must be invited in, it will not come through force. Brown Mamas who lead lives marked by peace, inside and out, are beacons for loving relationships. This does not mean they will not kiss frogs, but what it does mean is that Brown Mamas with a mindset for peaceful living, will create environments where only love can flourish.

A Brown Mama whose home is one of peace, concentrated effort and warmth, will not tolerate men who want chaotic houses they can run in and out of. Moreover, this type of man will not be comfortable in the peaceful environment she has created.

Mamas who possess a Brown Mama Mindset regarding love, won't fall for the trick of flowers and a fancy car on the first date. She understands that a man who buys her winter socks, pays her light bill or picks the kids up from school, is seeking to fulfill her need for well-being, rather than impress her with gifts that merely delight the basic senses.

Those with the Brown Mama Mindset are not easily fooled by materialism. We understand the value of being in charge of our inner-being rather than being in control of our relationship, and are ready and willing to meet the vibrational energy required to engage in an internally fulfilling relationship.

If you haven't met the water to your seed yet, that's okay because you lack nothing. Rather than focusing on finding love, be love. Love is peace. Peace is Joy. Joy is love.

Complementarity

Sometimes the best relationships are created by two people who just want to win. Two people who could care less *who* makes the money or *who* puts the kids to bed, but are more focused on making the money and getting the kids in the bed in the first place, typically meet their goals.

Those type of relationships last longer and are much happier because the individuals participating don't care who is leading the win, as long as THEY are winning.

For the first 10 years of my marriage I always felt like we were winning. For 7 out of our first 10 years of marriage my husband had a six-figure job. I've been a stay at home parent since we met (minus 2 spotty years of work), and my kids were very well taken care of. In my mind we were winning.

I always thought that the next step for our family would be entrepreneurship. Owning a business would certainly be the next step toward cementing our relationship and passing down a legacy of ownership to our children. I prayed that one day my husband would be able to quit his job, and we'd be able to begin a new journey toward complete self-sufficiency.

I had no idea that would happen in year 10, and I had no idea it would require me to stretch so far, and sacrifice so much.

The first 10 years of my marriage was spent getting comfortable with my husband. I'm pretty sure the next 10 years will be marked by our ability, or inability, to complement one another.

I first encountered the term "complementarity" in a book written by Mwalimu K. Bomani Baruti by that same name. In the book he defines "complementarity" as: "Two differently qualified, yet intimately interacting beings, forces or things diligently and continuously working toward a healthy, wholistic balance."

This definition could not be any more relevant than in the current season of our relationship. In this new quest toward entrepreneurship, we've both been challenged to use our differing skillsets and personalities to move our family business forward with diligence, consistency and hard work.

This means he has to trust me to do the accounting, and I have to trust him to make executive decisions when it comes to dealing with business partnerships. It also means that he might have to cook dinner some nights while I'm typing away at the computer, and I may have to sit at soccer games in the cold while he attends a class on team building.

Rather than be obsessed with who is leading the win, we have to continuously work toward the win even when we are uncomfortable with the position one of us may be temporarily playing.

Being a complementary couple is all about recognizing and playing off of your mate's strengths, while managing, and sometimes pulling extra weight, to compensate for one another's weaknesses.

The real growth in a relationship occurs when you accept your mate for who he is, and learn to interact with him in a way that inspires and assists him in becoming the best version of himself. This will require sacrifice.

Being a complement to your man is all about sacrificing some of your disagreeable characteristics, in order that you might align your strengths with your mate's strengths to produce a stronger vibrational pull toward your shared desires.

Many times, what couples are referring to when they speak of being "completed" by their mates, is the alignment of their unique degree of agreeability with their mate's unique degree of agreeability to create a whole, 360-degree relationship that is able to approach the world from a more holistic vantage point.

Being a complement means realizing that co-dependency is a natural state of being. In fact, being a complement means understanding that humans operate from a more natural state when we are reliant upon each other.

Trusting partnerships in which each member flourishes as a result of their shared reliance on one another's strengths, create long-lasting and powerful alliances that can be replicated by our children, and looked upon by our community as beacons of productivity and unity for years to come.

Mama Map Invitation

This invitation will complement the work you did in your *Mama Map Workbook* in Chapter 11. This time we will use our workbook to materialize our perfect mate.

Chapter 14

Parenting the Black Way

"It is not enough to fill African children with knowledge. It must be knowledge that is appropriate, it must be knowledge that is relevant to solving the problems of African people."
-Amos Wilson

Realizing that I was not parenting the *Black Way* was a hard pill to swallow. It was a semi-ordinary morning. I'd been toying around with what homeschooling might look like in my house after listening to a webinar where a former teacher talked about the success she had homeschooling her sons.

That morning this thought weighed heavily on my mind. I reluctantly got the boys dressed and ready for school. We piled into the car on that fall day and blasted Bob Marley during our 15- minute ride, which was our morning tradition. When we got to the school I coincidentally was able to get the good parking spot. Parents loved parking in this spot because you could see all the way up to the first-floor staircase and wave goodbye to your kids as they reached the final step. I kissed my two younger sons goodbye, and sat gazing at the staircase. I waited for them to reach the top step. As they approached the top, an unknown teacher greeted them.

I scanned his face and body language wondering what he was saying to my sons. Had they run too fast up the steps? Was there an emergency? Who was this man? In that moment, I realized one thing: I did not know this teacher.

I'd never seen his face or heard his voice and part of me wondered if he was a teacher at all. I was uncomfortable and something in my soul jumped. I didn't *know* him.

He wasn't the only teacher in the school that I didn't know. Of course, the school had over 30 teachers and I couldn't know all of them, but it suddenly hit me that during the course of my sons' 7-hour school day, they were surrounded by people who I didn't know well at all.

I'd never been to their homes. Didn't know their families. I had no idea what their political or religious ideologies were or what opinions they'd formed growing up. Despite being the PTA president, I'd never had a serious conversation that centered on shared cultural beliefs, or the lack thereof, with anyone at the school. Most conversations centered on educational achievement, expectations and, occasionally, educational current news or topics. But, I didn't *know* them.

On top of that, I was slightly frustrated with myself that I'd never bothered to have these conversations. It was enough that the vast majority of my sons' teachers didn't share the same gender, race, class or even neighborhood as they did.

But in addition to that I began to ask myself questions like, what might their teachers think about the politics of race, poverty and gender in America? Were their teachers choosing books and learning material that showed them the greatness of Blacks in

America and beyond, or were they choosing books that maintain the American legacy of oppression of people of color? How were my boys being taught science, history and reading comprehension? *Who* were they being taught these subjects for? Were their teacher's intentions for their lives different from my own? Were their minds being filled with information for information sake, or were they being prepared to take on the world as Black men at the bottom of the totem pole who must work their way to the top.

I began to question the method of parenting I had chosen. Moreover, I began to question whether my boys' current reality was preparing them to leap our family forward out of the generational curses that have kept my family in poverty, or the opposite.

3 Methods of Parenting

In the book, *The Warrior Method*, Dr. Raymond Winbush lays down a foundation for Black parents seeking to raise African-centered, community-driven and culturally conscious Black boys. One of the most poignant themes that runs through his book is the idea that African-American parents have an unconscious acceptance of racism that typically derives from unquestioned parenting such as what I was engaging in. I think this unconscious acceptance is extremely commonplace among Black parents.

Further, Winbush says there are 3 ways you can parent.

The first is the *White Way*, which is characterized by Black parents who have accepted racial imbalance and discrimination in the world and seek to help their children become *immune* to it.

White Way parents commonly say things to their kids like, "you just have to jump a little higher and run a little faster to be as good as everyone else." You might hear *White Way* parents tell their kids that racism is "just the way it is". *White Way* parents prepare their children for a life of discrimination and tell them there is no way around it except to do better. In fact, many *White Way* parents actually believe that going to college and getting a good job is a real way to overcome racism and *beat the system.*

Winbush says there is also a *Grey Way* of parenting. The *Grey Way* is marked by reactions to racism, but a continued unconscious acceptance. *Grey Way* parents usually do a great job making teachers and administrators accountable for their actions. Just like *White Way* parents, *Grey Way* parents make sure their kids have *the best.*

They go to PTA Meetings, attend every parent teacher conference, enroll their kids in every extra-curricular activity possible and, overall, just go to bat for their kids. Just like *White Way* parents, *Grey Way* parents are preparing their kids to overcome racism by any means necessary.

However, these parents also have deficit thinking ingrained in their brains. Although they are willing to fight racism and are the first parents to go to school and fight on behalf of any injustice, they still honestly believe that western education is the only way for their kids to elevate above oppression. Most Black parents fall into this category. Either they don't know the *Black Way* exists, or they believe there are too many barriers to parenting the *Black Way*.

But, a few parents are able to transition from the *Grey Way* to the *Black Way* of parenting. Winbush explains that *Black Way* parents have also committed to excellence on all front, BUT they are choosing to remove all interferences that impede upon filling the minds of African children with knowledge that is essential to solving the problems of African people.

These are typically parents who send their children to African-centered or cultural schooling environments, homeschool or build their own schools. These parents are committed to creating children who are culturally aware, and more importantly, culturally ready to help in the fight to take back Black communities. *Black Way* parents are committed to assisting Black children as they become Black adults capable of solving the problems of Black people in order that they might inherit the wealth that Black people are capable of cultivating.

Now of course, children raised the *Grey Way* and *White Way* are perfectly capable of assisting in the redevelopment of Black communities and may even excel there.

However, when it comes to re-imagining new possibilities for Black communities it will be necessary to have adults that don't feel even a tinge of racial inferiority, status quo compliance, or unconscious acceptance of cultural norms that are often derived from parenting practices passed down through the *Grey and White Way* parenting styles.

The children who will create the new Black community will need to be reared learning about the trials African people have faced, studying the defeats we have endured and developing new strategies for overcoming our current problems.

Parents engaged in *Black Way* parenting are raising children who will focus intensely on these ideals versus parenting styles that prioritize mainstream success and place solving Black problems in the peripheral of their children's lives.

I felt this unconscious acceptance and *Grey* style of parenting send a chill through my body the day that I realized I'd been getting my children dressed daily, packing their bags, kissing them goodbye and handing them off to people that, not only did I not know, but that I could not see.

Can She See Your Child?

In the wildly popular sci-fi movie, the Avatar, the Na'vi (also known in American culture as the blue people) greeted each other with a phrase: "Oel ngati kameie." This phrase would translate into English as "I see you."

In the movie it is revealed that this greeting was a way for the people of Pandora to express their shared culture. They were literally saying to each other that they had 20/20 vision into one another's pains, joys, loves, hurts, daily routine and other aspects of life that run along the same lines when people share a common culture.

In the Warrior Method, Raymond Winbush speaks of the importance of a shared culture between teacher and child.

Children learn best, feel better and are empowered more when they can see themselves as one with their environment. When there is a seamless integration between learning and a child's daily life and culture, the mind is easily stimulated and enhanced.

I began homeschooling my boys in 2016 and this truth was something I understood after just one year of doing so.

Any mother who's ever taught her child anything, knows that context makes all the difference. For example, when testing, a Black child may fair better when asked to describe a trip to her grandmother's house than she may when asked to describe her family's vacation last summer. If she is anything like the average Black child, she may, or may not, have gone on a family vacation last summer.

When I teach my sons about the Black Panthers and they can see someone with their same skin color who is fierce, determined and supremely intellectual, they get excited.

When they find out that their favorite comic book was written by someone who lives down the street from us or in a neighborhood that looks and feels just like ours, it makes their own dreams of writing or drawing seem a little bit closer.

As the president of the PTA at my sons' former school, I often saw the miscommunication of cultural cues between Black students and their white teachers.

From white teachers "fixing" a little Black girl's hair, to asking Black students where they went on summer vacation, to the ever present "Black boy savior" that exists in many white female teachers who coddle Black boys assuming they are in constant danger even from their parents. Have we ever stopped to ask how our children are interpreting these crossed cultural cues?

What message does it send to the little Black girl when her hair has to be "fixed?" What emasculating tendencies are we enhancing in our sons when they are viewed as needing to be "saved" from their homes, communities and even us, their mothers? Are we doing our children any justice by allowing them to not only spend 7+ hours per day with people we don't know, but allowing them to learn the fundamentals of life from people who have historically oppressed the true story of African people?

And, this is not just my opinion. The educational institutions of the status quo second this understanding.

A 2012 University of Pittsburgh study entitled *Parental Racial Socialization as a Moderator of the Effects of Racial Discrimination* published in the journal *Child Development* showed African-American children learn best when their parents engage in racial socialization practices with them.

These racial socialization practices were summarized as activities that promote pride in one's cultural or ethnic identity. Children whose parents "racially socialized" them experienced better academic achievement, positive cognitive engagement, and higher educational aspirations.

This study, and many others conducted prior to it, prove that there is no achievement gap in America there is only a culture gap.

If we know that 'racial socialization' and pride in one's culture increases the chances for academic success, then why do we leave it as a task to be done at home when home is where children spend the least amount of time every day, and school is where they spend the most?

The task of implementing African and African-American pride in academia should be massive and swift to ensure we don't unnecessarily lose another generation of our children to low achievement. It's not enough that white teachers begin teaching our kids about Malcolm X.

Mothers with a Brown Mama Mindset realize it is our responsibility to culturally equip our kids with not only the knowledge, but the confidence to live a life as the successor of cultivated Black wealth.

WE are what is required to close this cultural gap. Brown Mamas are the drum beat whose rhythm our children will dance to. We must begin to reject the status quo of what it means to be educated as an African-American in America. As the infamous intellectual Amos Wilson said: "It is not enough to fill African children with knowledge. It must be knowledge that is appropriate, it must be knowledge that is relevant to solving the problems of African people."

Parenting the *Black Way* needs to be given its own kind of significance and importance. It needs to mean that we not only fight to ensure our children master ABCs and 123s, but that we begin to help them become problem solvers of the issues that tear down the communities Brown Mamas step foot into every day.

What better way to solve our neighborhood problems than to raise the problem solvers ourselves.

Mamas with a Brown Mama Mindset will raise their children to

- Recognize and appreciate all African history at an early age
- Value the communities we live in and work to make them better
- Properly handle their financial, material, cognitive and collective resources

- Teach our girls to be superior mothers, wives and scholars
- Raise our sons with the expectation of marriage and scholarship. Raise our sons to protect the girls and women in our communities
- Develop institutions that insulate, educate and instill confidence in our children

In short, parenting with a Brown Mama Mindset is all about preparing your children to develop new, positive and sustainable realities, not just for our Brown Babies today, but also for the Brown Babies of the future.

Black Kid Magic?

Evidence throughout the years has shown that Black children, although born into more plight and trial than other ethnic groups in America, learn and develop at a much faster pace than their counterparts.

As homeschooling takes root in Black America, we see it more and more. Black children who become violin aficionados, learn 100 languages or start million-dollar businesses before they turn 10. These stories and images are brandished with #blackgirlmagic and #brownboymagic. But, is it really magic at all?

In the book *Awakening the Genius of the Black Child* by Amos Wilson, evidence is put forth to show that Black children lift their heads, roll over, crawl, walk, are ready for solid foods and even talk at a much younger age than their Caucasian counterparts.

Wilson quotes a 1970 study researched and written by American pediatrician and clinical psychologist Arnold Gesell.

The study reported remarkable differences in the physical and psychological development of Black children. A study of children in Uganda and the Caribbean showed that at two days-old Black children were capable of balancing their own heads and focusing their eyes. These same developmental milestones were not reached in American white children until 6 weeks old.

The same study showed that while an American white child would not sit up by themselves until 24 weeks-old, a Black Jamaican child could sit up on his own by 6 weeks-old.

Outside of this study, I have experienced these early developmental milestones in my own children. My oldest son began talking, in full words, by the time he was 10 months old. My two younger children were both walking by 9 months old.

For us Brown Mamas, this is nothing remarkable as we were all raised being told by our grandmothers that our children would develop a little faster than what the white doctors would view as normal.

But, what we have not been able to do is question all of the other developmental milestones that have been set for Black children that are based on mainstream development standards.

If we know, from the raising and rearing or our own children, that our brown babies developmentally exceed the milestones of our white counterparts, then why do we allow white education professionals to create standards of learning for our children that may not be in line with what is necessary for their proper development?

Who made the rule that the only way to learn is to sit in front of a teacher for 6 hours and do worksheets? Are these effective learning tools, or would Black children's minds be better suited for audible, interactive or kinesthetic learning styles?

Who set the milestone that all children must read by second grade, or be deemed incompetent? Science has proven that for males, both white and Black, this might not be a realistic learning timeline.

Has anyone asked the question: What is appropriate for Black children? Why is it not okay for children of differing ethnicities, cultures and environmental makeup to think and learn differently? Especially considering these children are born, raised and reared in different environments with parents of differing statuses and substance and, with different expectations and communal needs.

Wilson makes the point that education then for Black children must grow to include learning that occurs in a fundamentally different environment than the slower paced and, often sedentary education currently developed and administered by white America (we know that 82 percent of school teacher and administrators in America are white, over 70 percent are white women).

Many Brown Mamas are beginning to ask these questions and in droves, exploring different options to homeschool their children. Black families have grown to make up 10 percent of all homeschooled children as of 2015 according to the National Home Education Research Institute.

This homeschooling movement goes beyond whether or not Black children are indeed magic, and goes into the sphere of Brown Mamas redefining what it means for Black children to be 'educated'.

Many of us Mamas are realizing that a sacrifice must be made if we are to leave a legacy of *real* Black excellence to our grandchildren.

Reality is, Real Love = Sacrifice

In order to master a Brown Mama Mindset, this type of sacrifice is not only necessary, but needs to be an honored tradition. Moms with a Brown Mama Mindset are prepared to ask the hard questions and take on the real responsibility of sacrificing our own comfort and wants for the emotional, intellectual and developmental needs of our children.

While Black children may be innately blessed with physical attributes and intellectual valor, Black parenting is not magic. Reality is talent and intelligence are just part of Black Kid Magic. The other half is hard work, perseverance, discipline and mental fortitude. These are all skills that are ignited by good parenting.

The problem is what we are igniting at home is often being torn down in the world. It is being impeded upon when the Black excellence and pride that we are igniting at home is not being echoed at school where our children spend the majority of their time.

Oftentimes, we become so focused on what we want our children to *do* in the world, that we forget to really hone in on who they are *becoming* in the world. Who your child will be is far more important than what they will do.

That begs the question, who are our children becoming if they are, in fact, being mentally stagnated in American educational institutions? What kinds of lives will our children be forced into if we continue to ignore the effects this type of lifestyle is having on our children.

And, if we are stunting our children's mental and emotional growth and health by sending them to institutions that are not accurately assessing and developing their mental capabilities, we must begin to ask ourselves how much we are really expressing genuine care and concern for them.

One of my favorite Brown Mamas set out on a journey to homeschool her children as a single mom two years ago. She's been asked many times how she did it. Every time she replies with the same answer. She says, "I had to decide who was going to make the sacrifice. Either I was going to make the sacrifice, or my children were going to **be** the sacrifice."

Just like this Brown Mama did, we have to rise to the occasion and present our children with the opportunity to really express their inner greatness and magic.

This starts by ensuring that each day they are being surrounded by folks who believe in their ability to be magical children.

Will They See the Monsters?

Some days part of our homeschooling curriculum includes watching movies. We watch movies and write about them, dissect them and see if we can find parallels to everyday life.

One week we watched the awesome movie *Ms. Peregrine's Home for Peculiar Children*. It was a great movie with some really timely messages for Black families.

The main character, Jake, was a peculiar child, who didn't know he possessed super powers. He ends up entering into a world where he visits a home for children with superpowers only to find out he also possessed them.

His gift was the ability to see the monsters that had been chasing the super kids for decades. He went on an adventure with his new friends and ended up getting separated from them.

When Jack is separated from his friends he worries about their fate and becomes disheartened about whether his friends will survive. His road back to his friends was marked by some awesome advice from his grandfather. He told his grandad he did not know where his friends were going, so he couldn't find them. His grandfather responded,

"Ah! But, you know where they've been!"

With this advice Jake found his way back to his super friends.

The Brown Mama Mindset

When the movie was over I thought about what parenting really means for Mamas with a Brown Mama Mindset.

It means giving your children a road map that details where they've been so they will be able to see the monsters of their past and predict the location and actions of the monsters of their present and future.

Mama, if you don't have a thorough understanding of your past it is almost impossible for you to see the monsters of your present and future. All the mainstream, science, math, art and reading in the world will not prepare *our* children to take on the monsters that for hundreds of years have stalked African-American people.

Likewise, even though all of the children at the peculiar house had super powers like flying and throwing fire, without Jake's ability to see the monsters they were lost. The children couldn't evade or destroy monsters that they could not see.

Mamas with a Brown Mama Mindset give their children eyes that demystify the monsters of poverty and racism, and replace them with the eye-opening powers of racial confidence, responsible management of resources and collective economics and empowerment.

Mothers that possess a Brown Mama mindset will not make the mistake of educating their children in the ways of western society without raising them within a lifestyle of Black excellence and giving them a blueprint for creating uniquely Black traditions and rituals.

Brown Mama Mindset masters are not focused on what their children will *do* in life, we are focused on who are children are becoming in the present and the legacy they will leave in the future.

As Brown Mamas we possess a unique history and worthy perspective that should be first, not last, in our children's minds as they go on to raise and rear the Brown Mamas of the next generation.

Mama Map Invitation

If you can see it, you can achieve it. Use your Mama Map Workbook to create the community of your dreams.

Chapter 15

Sankofa

"It is never taboo to go back and fetch what is lost." -Sankofa

I remember the second time I lost a part of my true self. I was about 8 years-old. I lived right across the street from the school that I attended at the time. As a child I was small, skinny and shy around unfamiliar people. School was never my favorite place to be. Mostly because I was constantly surrounded by people who I had no familiarity with; even at a young age I knew this was not my preference.

One such person was a very tall, husky girl named Tiff. Tiff was the biggest girl in my class. Most kids were afraid of her. I'd never thought about being afraid of Tiff because I never thought about Tiff. When I was in school I spent most of my time daydreaming and trying my best to redirect everyone's attention away from me. As a child, I never wanted to be the center of attention. I preferred to pass the time doing my schoolwork until recess, where I could reunite with my sisters and cousin who also attended the school.

I still don't remember why Tiff wanted to fight me, but I'm pretty sure it had something to do with her entering my personal space. Although I was a skinny, shy kid at school, I was always fiercely protective of my personal space. That meant that I didn't want to be touched and I treated my sisters and cousin like they were my lion cubs. If you touched them, there was no question, I had to fight you.

But Tiff was big.

She was really, really big. At 9 years-old she towered over all the kids in the class, even the boys, like a skyscraper awkwardly seated next to a pizza shop.

When she decided that we were going to fight one day after school, I decided the only logical thing for me to do was to run. I only lived across the street, and I was little and fast. So that's what I did. That day before the rooting of "Fight! Fight!" could even materialize, I jetted out the school door and across the street to my two-story apartment building. I slammed the door behind me *and* hid behind my bedroom door.

My mom came out of nowhere. I didn't even know she was home. She was usually at work during this time of day. She asked me why I ran home and why I was hiding behind my bedroom door.

I told her that Tiff chased me home and that Tiff was big. She was really, really big.

Before we get to the next part, I need to tell you that I did not grow up in a good neighborhood. I grew up in Wilkinsburg. At that time the LAW gang was running Wilkinsburg and the apartment we lived in was dead smack in the middle of their territory. I'm an 80s baby so it was about 1989, and it seemed most inner-cities in the U.S. were in the middle of a violent, destructive crack epidemic. My mom was one of the few parents I know of who wasn't smoking crack.

In my neighborhood many kids were roaming the streets unparented. The kids who *did* have parents, or *a* parent, that wasn't smoking crack, were lucky. Even those of us who came home to meals, had parents who paid the bills and checked our homework, had to learn how to survive in the neighborhood. That meant we had to learn to keep the doors locked when our parents weren't home, to never take anything from strangers who offered and we had to learn how to fight.

For that reason, when my mom found out that I'd ran from Tiff and that the entire school had watched, she made me go defend myself. She spoke the historic Black mom words, "Either you fight her, or you fight me." I chose the former.

I was shook. I went back outside trembling. I just knew that I was going to return home in 30 minutes with a busted lip, broken arm or in a body bag. Tiff was waiting for me.

The crowd of elementary school kids formed with Big Tiff and scrawny Muffy in the middle. The next thing that happened was both hilarious, and life changing for me.

Big Tiff tussled me, shaken baby style. She put her long, copper tone arms on my arms and started shaking me around. I thought to myself, "Is this all she's got?" I bit her as hard as I could on her forearm and she buckled gripping her arm in pain. Then I jumped on her and started going HAM! Next thing I knew, everyone was cheering me on and Tiff was walking home with her bookbag dragging on the ground, gripping her arm and crying.

My dad taught me how to bite someone properly when I was a little girl, and that day, the lesson paid off. It proved an effective strategy in the many fights that would follow my tussle with Big Tiff, and there were a lot.

From that day on, I stopped being the shy, scared Muffy and became the Muffy who could fight.

You may be thinking that this new disposition benefitted me. It certainly should have kept other kids from bothering me and allowed me to resume my peaceful life at school. Even I thought that it would scare kids off and cause them to leave me alone for the rest of the school year. After all, I was the one who held the title of beating up the biggest girl in my class.

But, no. That was not the case. That was not the kind of environment I lived in.

In a neighborhood full of broken homes and aggressive children looking for an outlet due to the lack of care and concern they were receiving at home, I became a trophy to be won.

The kids in my class now wanted their turn to beat up the 'biggest kid in class', which was now me. That school year I got into 5 fights. The next school year, many more. I lost most of those fights. By 5th grade, my mom had been to the school so many times they should have given her a plaque for most involved parent.

Even worse, my self-esteem took a deep, deep dive. With every fight, my exterior became more hardened and fierce, but internally I was confused, hurt and unsure of who I was becoming. I wasn't a kid who liked to fight. I was a kid who wanted to make friends. I was a kid who loved writing and reading; an intelligent introvert. Instead of school being a vehicle to help me climb further out of my shell, I became afraid to even participate during class time because every bit of attention I received seemed to be negative attention.

I tried so hard to make myself invisible during those school years, but no matter what, my reputation preceded me and I just couldn't seem to stop fighting. A fire ignited in me, a fire that I still possess today. It's a fire that I am proud of and that has made me who I am, but it is not ALL of me.

That was the problem. When I was a kid, I became a fighter. Being the person who everyone wanted to fight defined the totality of my personality. Seemingly overnight, I transformed from shy, nearly invisible Muffy into Street Fighter Muffy.

Through numerology and astrology, I've learned that fire is actually the element that my personality defaults too. Opinionated, fierce and bold are some of the words that have come to describe my nature over the years. And, I LOVE this side of me.

The problem is not in the aggressiveness that I exhibited that school year, as it is innately a part of my persona. The problem is that I was not able to make the decision to debut that part of my personality.

I was never given the time to decide how or when I wanted the more aggressive side of my personality to surface. At that moment my life became a part of the dream of the world. I was no longer in control of defining who I wanted to be, the pull of someone else's reality had sucked me in and I was forced to adapt, for better or worse.

Unconscious Agreements

Can you relate? So many of us Brown Mamas are living in a world that we did not agree to.

Erykah Badu says it so well in her song "Certainly." She said, "Who gave you permission to rearrange me, certainly not me".

So many of us Mamas are living out realities that we never decided on. We are raising children having never decided upon a real strategy, or even lifestyle, for rearing children. We are working jobs that we feel we have no choice but to be enslaved to. We are in relationships that have control over our emotions and mindset, and we feel stuck.

While we may not feel like we've had a choice, the truth is we have made agreements in our lives that we've felt uncomfortable with and have had to live through the consequences.

Even at 8-years-old, I made decisions that day. I decided to run from Big Tiff. I decided to rise to the occasion of the applause I received for being a fighter. Although I may not have made a conscious agreement, the agreement was there nonetheless.

Many of us have unconsciously decided we are unworthy of peace, love, joy and financial wellness. We constantly play out these disagreeable agreements in our minds and they manifest in our reality.

Oftentimes we don't know we are making the agreements because just like me on the day I fought Big Tiff, we allow the world's definition of who we are to define us.

Even when we are uncomfortable with the world's new definition of ourselves, we are swooned by its applause. As a result, we slowly, agreement by agreement, melt further into the world's dream until who we really are is a distant memory, and we are now trapped by the personality our friends, family members and world has given us.

But, there is a way out.

STOP and GO BACK!

The African teaching of Sankofa is a beautiful concept. Through the Sankofa saying "It is never taboo to go back and fetch what is lost", we are reminded that we cannot go far into the future if we are not first aware of where we've been. Taking the Sankofa concept even further, one could say that we cannot inherit the promises of the future until we heal the wounds of the past.

Five years ago, I decided to stop. Instead of moving forward in brokenness, I decided to stop and become whole. I prayed. I fasted. I meditated, and cried for days sometimes. I went back into my past, and told scared, afraid and aggressive Muffy that no one was out to get her and that she could come out of the shell.

I read the Bible, countless African history books on philosophy, social justice, culture and everything in between. I joined the PTA and went to my kids' schools and began a journey to get to know them. I stopped yelling at my husband and started listening to him, and even better I started seeing him.

I gardened. Oh, how I fell in love with the Earth! I realized that the healing I was searching for was not in my career, or in travelling or in shopping or even in friendships. The healing I was searching for was in quiet, in stillness, in being one with the Earth that had joined with the soul of the Creator to bring forth a life as humble as mine.

I went back to fetch what I had lost. I went back to fetch ME.

Right now, *you've* got to decide to stop. Stop everything. You must stop because everything that you are currently engaging in that does not come from a place of wholeness is coming from a place of brokenness.

Stopping is not easy. It's not easy to stop working a job that feeds your family, but is killing your soul. It's not easy to admit you may be failing your children. It's not easy to take responsibility for the parts of your relationships that are screwed up. It's not easy to see yourself for who you have *really* become, because so much of who you have become is **not** who you really are.

You need to stop so that you can go back and fetch what you lost. You lost YOU. The concept of Sankofa is often used to describe the need African people have to go back and find our pre-slavery roots, but the concept of Sankofa is also one Brown Mamas need to use in their everyday lives.

In the context of today's modern Mama, we need to go back and fetch our original selves. While there is certainly a need for every Black woman to review her past in order to forge an ordered and sensible future, it is of equal importance that every Brown Mama return to the root of her childhood to fetch the origins of who she is.

Who were you before that fight? Who were you before he, or she, touched you? Who were you before mom and dad broke up? Who were you before it happened?

Just like I did, go back to that first moment where you had the first thought that you needed to be someone other than who you really are. Examine that moment and experience by asking yourself:

How did I feel in that moment?

What new personality, or characteristics sprang up in me as a result of this newly made agreement?

What realities am I currently facing as a result of the agreements I've made since then?

These are questions you must explore with true authenticity. There is no better person to be yourself with than YOU. Admit that you've abused yourself. Admit that you haven't been a good steward of your own heart. Admit that you allowed yourself to be taken advantage of.

And, it's okay, cause it's just you here. You're not going to tell anybody AND you're NOT going to judge yourself because you deserve to be able to be honest with someone.

This is the thing Mama, you've got to ask yourself, 'Do I want to make any more decisions that are predicated on what I've lost?'

So, go ahead sis, let it all hang out on the inside. Sankofa is your divine right as a woman of African descent.

Stop that new business venture that's driving you crazy, stop forcing your kids into all those extracurricular activities that leave you with no time to clear your mind or see them smile. Stop running to the night club every weekend. JUST STOP.

Stop, go back and fetch **you**. You deserve to take every step of every day from a place of peace, from a place of love and from a place of joy. Wholeness is your natural state of well-being.

Looking Forward,
Muffy Mendoza

Reflections

I. An Homage to Home

It's so easy to take your home for granted. Home has become the place that we come back to. It's become a stop on our journey of life. For Black mothers in particular, home has become a place we long to get away from. Previously, I've hoped to only see my home in the rearview mirror. I've dreamed of distant lands I might travel to. My home would serve only as a backdrop for gathering luggage or as a pit stop for checking on my family and children in those dreams. During these fantasies the intricacies of home just didn't seem that important. In my longing for anything other than my current circumstances, I didn't realize how much the concept of home had molded me. How even the color of walls, feeling of an entryway, texture of a hardwood floor, or carpet underneath my feet added to the depth and color of every moment of my life. I didn't realize that home was not just a part of my life, but the epicenter of my life.

In my haste to make plans to leave home, I forgot how beautiful it is to walk into my dining room and see the flood of morning light that brings to life the mahogany wood table where my family has eaten so many birthday, anniversary and just everyday dinners together. The table where my father counseled me and my husband's marriage back to health on countless occasions. In my quickness to get a life, I had forgotten that I am a life. I forgot that my life had been created bedroom by bedroom, vase by vase, dresser by dresser the same way my mother designed her home with care and concern. I forgot that the walls of my mother's home talked every day in the words I speak, actions I engage in and the way in which I treat others. My mother's walls talked all through my life. It was just up to me to hear what they were saying.

When I finally listened, when I finally awoke and was interested in what my mother's walls had to say they said one thing in a crystal-clear whisper my mother's walls told me: "Go Home."

Reflections

They spoke with such clarity, with such intent and with such substance, that I obliged.

Over the past ten years of life I've embarked on a journey to stop taking my homelife for granted. I still enjoy a good vacation, but I'm most happy painting walls, redesigning wreaths for each season and watching my kids run through my house making messes. (Well that doesn't make me happy, but it certainly adds spice to our family story.) I've decided to stop prioritizing the peripheral of my life and work on the interior; because you best believe that being fulfilled at home is all about being fulfilled on the inside. When you begin the journey to get ya homelife, skeletons are going to come out of your closets (literally and figuratively), dust bunnies of the past will begin to jump out of your soul and you'll begin to see life just as clearly as windows after Windex.

When I began to not just live in, but, enjoy my home the sun came out. Because for women, our homes are our solace. Your home is the place where you set about intention for other aspects of your life. Your home is where you meditate and send prayers of purpose that activate the universe. I can't count how many times the lamp on my nightstand has stayed awake with me worrying about family members, my husband, my life. It has been faithful; only occasionally asking for a new bulb. My kitchen has been so gracious to me; offering hot food and space where only women can tell secrets of life, love and virtues of "the Lord" as my mama says.

What I know for sure (as Oprah would say) is that home is faithful. When I think about the Bible and how it constantly described God as the great "I AM," I think about the constant things of life. The things that never fail us like the sun, wind, grass, flowers, trees, rain and love. But, more often than not, I also find myself thinking about home.

II. Mama 3:16

I want to kiss my kids with the wettest lips and hug them with the tightest grip

For all of the times my Mama dragged herself to work for eight plus hours so that I could have lights, heat, food and new school clothes even when she wanted

Reflections

to stay home and cuddle up with me and my sisters to watch movies or eat Bon-Bons

I want to be soft for my Mama.

I want to cook meals for my husband and sons that are colorful and nutritious
That are filled with love as I stir and blend with the thoughtfulness, kindness and joy of 200 Martha Stewarts

For all the times my mother made hot meals after long days.
For all the times we ate all the snacks and cereal and didn't save her any
And all the times she worked over-time so me and my sisters could get $20 to go to the mall and eat at the food court

I want to be soft for my Mama.

I want to have family over ALL the time.

The Brown Mama Mindset

I want to make sure that grandma, auntie, all my nieces and nephews and cousins are in the house together making good food and loving on each other. I want to make sure my husband is on the grill and that I greet him with a cup of ice water and a kiss...

For all of the times my mother made a dollar out of 15 cents and filled the Christmas tree with presents, looking on as we opened them with a smile, only to trek back to work the very next day...

I want to be soft for my Mama.

I want to take my kids to the park every day in the summer and play video games with them
I want to tickle them until they pee their pants and give them motherly advice until they frown
For all the times my mom took me and my sisters to the park, had Saturday morning conversations with us over eggs, bacon and toast in the kitchen and for every piece of advice she ever gave me

I want to be soft for my Mama.

Reflections

And finally, just like Biggie said, I wanna be soft for my Mama because she deserves a limousine with a sofa, mink on her back and to sip champagne when she's thirst-ay (no typo)!

I'm going to be soft because for too long my Mama, and your Mama too, had to be strong for sister, daddy, auntie, uncle, and everybody else.
I'm going to be soft because my mother deserves it. And the next best thing to having something for yourself, is having it for your children.

For Mama so loved us that she put on the strong face so we wouldn't have to.

Bibliography & Recommendations

The following books were used in the writing of *The Brown Mama Mindset* and are highly recommended as reading material for Black mothers everywhere.

Mckeown, Greg *Essentialism*. The Crown Publishing Group, 2014.

Boone, Sylvia Ardyn, *Radiance From the Waters.* Yale University Press, 1986

Ani, Marimba (Dana Richards), *Let The Circle Be UnBroken.* New Haven and London, Nkonimfo Publications, 1980, 1997

Crawford, Larry (Mwalimu K. Bomani Baruti), *Complementarity*. Georgia, Akoben House, 2004

Hewlett, Barry S., *Intimate Fathers.* Ann Arbor, The University of Michigan Press, 1992

Winbush, Raymond, *The Warrior Method.* Harper Collins Publisher, 2002

Wilson, Amos, *Awakening the Genius of the Black Child.* African World Infosystems, June 1992

Ruiz, Don Miguel, *The Four Agreements: A Practical Guide to Personal Freedom,* Amber Allen Publishing November 1997

Made in the USA
Lexington, KY
25 April 2019